The National Defense Intelligence College supports and encourages research on intelligence issues that distills lessons and improves Intelligence Community capabilities for policy-level and operational consumers

This series of Occasional Papers presents the work of faculty, students and others whose research on intelligence issues is supported or otherwise encouraged by the National Defense Intelligence College (NDIC) through its Center for Strategic Intelligence Research. Occasional Papers are distributed to Department of Defense schools and to the Intelligence Community, and unclassified papers are available to the public through the National Technical Information Service *(www.ntis.gov)*. Selected papers are also available through the U.S. Government Printing Office *(www.gpo.gov)*.

Proposed manuscripts for these papers are submitted for consideration to the NDIC Editorial Board. Papers undergo review by senior officials in Defense, Intelligence and occasionally civilian academic or business communities. Manuscripts or requests for additional copies of Occasional Papers should be addressed to Defense Intelligence Agency, National Defense Intelligence College, MC-X, Bolling AFB, Washington, DC 20340-5100.

This publication has been approved for unrestricted distribution by the Office of Freedom of Information and Security Review, Washington Headquarters Services.

This Occasional Paper highlights a unique theme explored by an NDIC student in pursuit of his Master of Science of Strategic Intelligence degree, and is adapted from his submitted thesis. It illustrates clearly that students at the College are urged to be innovative and creative in selecting their topics, and that controlled experimentation is encouraged by the faculty in aiding students to reach original and useful conclusions. The results of this research on a topic of high visibility in the popular culture at present (witness the public fascination with the "CSI" or "NCIS" genre of media programming) will likely have significant impact on the intelligence arena for many years.

The author of this Occasional Paper, Albert M. Cruz, can be reached for questions or comments at (850) 499-5327, or *hardsomenavydvr@yahoo.com*.

William.Spracher@dia.mil, Editor
Center for Strategic Intelligence Research

Occasional Paper Number Twelve

CRIME SCENE INTELLIGENCE
An Experiment in Forensic Entomology

Albert M. Cruz, Lieutenant, USN

National Defense Intelligence College

WASHINGTON, DC
November 2006

CONTENTS

FIGURES

Figures (Continued)

TABLES

APPENDIX

FOREWORD

LT Albert Cruz's forensic entomology/explosive (E2) scientific project proved to be cutting edge and groundbreaking science in the forensic community. His thorough research and original analysis included a newly found forensic/intelligence analytical tool which could help bring justice, fight the war on terrorism, and find "ground truth" in cases which involve domestic and international terrorism, war crimes, torture, drug trafficking, and chemical explosive identification by utilizing the common carrion fly. In addition, the project may be effective in counter-denial and deception operations which are known to be highly relevant and valuable to the Intelligence Community (IC) in cases of deceptive mass grave movement and genocide.

More importantly, this unique forensic E2 experimental project revealed that explosive compounds such as TNT *could* be detected biologically — in this case by blowfly larvae which have fed on body tissue exposed to explosive residues — when toxicological analysis was no longer procurable. The results of the unique E2 forensic experiment provided empirical evidence that forensic entomology is unbiased and has a high degree of applicability to the IC. The science here is very helpful and when applied strategically to international war crime cases can provide myriad answers and help bring the guilty to justice in any war crime tribunal court system. Such information gained would also enable analysts to identify a specific batch of explosive, compare it to a known source of TNT, and relate it to a terrorist crime or cell.

This original study is remarkable. LT Cruz has provided a new model of explosive fingerprinting by utilizing the common insect. He has provided an outstanding "step by step" product for the intelligence and forensic communities. It is clear he has stepped "out of the box" and paved the way for future forensic intelligence experts by providing a valuable future tool which can offer answers to help fill valuable intelligence gaps in fighting the war on terrorism and crimes against humanity.

William C. Rodriguez III, Ph.D.
Chief, Deputy Medical Examiner
Office of the Armed Forces Medical Examiner
Rockville, Maryland

CRIME SCENE INTELLIGENCE

Forensic entomology is the study of how insects consume decomposing human remains and provide data which can aid medical/legal investigations. Common questions answered through the use of forensic entomology include time since death, movement of a body from one location to another, determination of environmental conditions to which a body has been exposed, location of traumatic wound sites, identification of toxicological deaths, and location of drug trafficking. However, many sub-disciplines of forensic sciences, including forensic entomology, have not been commonly utilized by the Intelligence Community (IC) to help solve heinous war crimes. Moreover, the degree of the field's applicability to military and intelligence analysis is not known. To date, there are no forensic entomology intelligence analysts or scientists actively engaged in the area of explosive residue identification utilizing forensic entomology.

The forensic entomology discipline in the IC can shed light on the "ground truth" and give a viable estimate, without bias, of the perpetrator's or suspect's past actions in heinous human crimes. When studying entomology and methods by which insects breed, attack, escape, discover, or attract, we may continually ask ourselves whether the principles that govern deception use in nature apply to human conflict. Can some principles in nature be used to counter deception operations? Will identifying and applying these principles at crime scenes be valuable?

Some cases where forensic entomology could yield intelligence—"ground truth" regarding past crimes, to include "counter-deception"—is in the execution of a victim or victims, as well as evidence of torture, drugging, and postmortem movement of the body. Other cases include mass graves movement, genocide, and the identification of toxicological and explosive compounds.

In preparing this study, the author consulted IC professionals and personnel with various medical organizations. CDR George Ferris, an Explosive Ordnance Disposal (EOD) officer and Weapons Branch Chief at the Joint Intelligence Task Force for Combating Terrorism (JITF-CT), Defense Intelligence Agency (DIA);[1] Michael Fanning, Intelligence Analyst at the Hazardous Devices Response Unit, Federal Bureau of Investigation (FBI);[2] George Klapec, Forensic Chemist at the Bureau of Alcohol, Tobacco, and Firearms (ATF);[3] Dr. Robert D. Hall, Associate Vice Provost for Research at the University of Missouri and

---

[1] CDR George Ferris, USNR, Chief, Weapons Branch, Joint Intelligence Task Force for Combating Terrorism (JITF-CT), Defense Intelligence Agency (DIA); U.S. Navy Special Operations Officer, Explosive Ordnance Disposal (EOD), Washington, DC, telephone interview by author, 8 June 2004.

[2] Michael Fanning, Intelligence Analyst at the Federal Bureau of Investigation's (FBI) Hazardous Devices Response Unit, FBI Academy, Quantico, VA, telephone interview by author, 8 June 2004.

[3] George Klapec, Forensic Chemist at the Federal Bureau of Alcohol, Tobacco, and Firearms (ATF), Washington Office, Washington, DC, telephone interview by author, 8 June 2004.

member of the American Board of Forensic Entomology (ABFE);[4] and Dr. William C. Rodriguez III, Chief, Deputy Medical Examiner, Office of the Armed Forces Medical Examiner (AFME),[5] confirmed that carrion insects, in particular blowflies, may be a valuable tool for intelligence-gathering analysts and law enforcement investigators dealing with international crimes in the area of homicide, suicide, and untimely deaths from terrorist bombings.

Hypothetical example: A U.S.-operated Boeing 737 airliner goes down in a Central American tropical rain forest with a member of the U.S. Senate on board. Members of the IC—an intelligence and law enforcement task force (CIA, FBI, ATF, and AFME)—have been called upon to take over the investigation. All four agencies reach the crash site within a one-week time frame. They would like to ascertain if the plane crashed into the remotely located mountain due to mechanical failure or was exploded by an improvised explosive device (IED). In addition, they would like to identify if the U.S. Senator was killed prior to the explosion, which would reveal a deception and misdirect blame. Thus, the theory in this case is that forensic entomology could or would be able to reveal whether explosive residues were present on the deceased and could help estimate the Postmortem Interval (PMI, or estimated time of death) by analyzing the blowfly larvae and pupae.

Although this line of research has never been tried or implemented within the forensic entomology field, federal agencies have noted its potential to become an important tool that can help advance the science of explosive detection and identification. This is made possible due to blowfly larvae feeding on postmortem human tissue, tissue which may have been exposed to the chemical residues from a detonated IED. Past entomological studies which would back up this theory of transferability through larvae have involved human DNA and drug uptake in blowfly larvae. As Dr. Hall observed, "In past cases where a highly decomposed female body is examined for evidenced of rape, semen samples usually are not available. But maggots taken from the vaginal area can be valuable and reveal if the woman was sexually assaulted, given the presence of the perpetrator's seminal DNA in the maggots. This would place the accused at the scene of the crime, during or shortly after the time of death or assault."[6] The significance of this finding is that if human DNA can be passed to fly larvae via feeding, it is plausible that explosive residues can be absorbed by fly larvae. The relevance of such information would allow IC analysts and operators to detect and identify compounds in terrorist bombings when other means of identification are not available.

These forensic determinations are possible, but only if entomological evidence is recognized, properly collected, and sent to a professional entomological laboratory for analysis by a qualified forensic entomologist. IC members, who are intelligence and law enforcement officers, must become fully aware of the complex processes associated with

---

[4]   Robert D. Hall, Ph.D., J.D., Associate Vice Provost for Research, University of Missouri, and member of the American Board of Forensic Entomology, telephone interview by author, 8 June 2004.

[5]   William C. Rodriguez III, Ph.D., Chief, Deputy Medical Examiner, Office of the Armed Forces Medical Examiner (AFME), Rockville, MD, telephone interview by author, 8 June 2004.

[6]   Hall, telephone interview.

the decay process and the important role that insects play in the degradation of the human body. Investigators must understand the need for specimen collection and recording of other pertinent field data. If the proper steps are followed, it is possible for insects to reveal silently the information we need to solve some international crimes, including terrorist-related bombings.

WHAT WE KNOW

Literature specifically addressing forensic entomology is minimal. The detection of explosive compounds relating to arthropod feeding activity and metabolic absorption is not addressed.

Some literature does address how entomological evidence is controlled, collected, and disseminated to forensic scientists to help solve various domestic crimes.

WHAT WE CAN LEARN

Despite the potential of the relatively new science of forensic entomology, the dearth of intelligence derived from this discipline to solve war crimes is troubling. On the eve of the 21st century, nations seem no closer to stopping war and ethnic violence than at the beginning of the previous millennium. There is fresh optimism, however, that at the close of a war-stained century nations have found the collective will to deter and punish those who commit crimes against humanity. International criminal tribunal courts, located in Sierra Leone, East Timor, Kosovo, and Cambodia, to name just a few, have been established around the world to prosecute perpetrators and enforce the laws of basic human rights. Within these courts, new scientific methods involving forensic science are being employed to prosecute those who commit war crimes. Although forensic science is an applied science related to law and special investigations in dealing with technical data such as DNA analysis, it is clear that specific disciplines within forensic science have not been utilized to their full potential by the IC. Close analysis reveals it is an important analytical resource which needs to be utilized by both the IC and the international criminal tribunal court system to find "ground truth."

The Central Intelligence Agency (CIA), the Defense Intelligence Agency (DIA), the Federal Bureau of Investigation (FBI), the Bureau of Alcohol, Tobacco, and Firearms (ATF), the Department of State (DOS), and the Department of Defense (DOD) armed services—which, among others, comprise the IC—can learn a great deal from the field of forensic entomology by collecting and extracting fluids from insect larvae. This information could provide intelligence operators and analysts from all federal departments with an alternative method to detect explosive compounds, especially when technical machines such as bomb analyzers are not readily accessible or are unsuitable in certain field environments.

Lord and Berger divide the scope of forensic entomology into three general components—medico-legal, urban, and stored-product pests. The medico-legal system focuses on the criminal component of the legal system and deals with the carrion feeding insects that typically infest human remains. The urban aspect deals with the insects that affect man and his environment. This area has both civil and criminal components as urban pests may feed on the living and the dead. The damage caused by their feeding activity can produce marks and wounds on tissues that may be misinterpreted as resulting from human abuse. Urban pests are of great economic importance, and the forensic entomologist may become involved in civil proceedings resulting in monetary damages. Lastly, stored product insects are commonly found in foodstuffs, and the forensic entomologist may serve as an expert witness during both civil and criminal proceedings involving food contamination.[7]

The scope of this project focuses primarily on the first component, which is termed medico-legal entomology and is intended to give the reader a basic understanding of the development and life cycle of the green bottle blowfly. Furthermore, evidence is provided of the green blowfly's presence near the Washington, DC, coastal area. It is further demonstrated that evidence collected from a body discovered outdoors or indoors with insect infestation can lead intelligence analysts and law enforcement investigators to estimate the postmortem interval (PMI), probable cause of death, presence of drugging, postmortem movement of the body, and the detection of explosive compounds.

WHY USE INSECTS?

Why use insects? Although the exact species of fauna may differ from country to country, from habitat to habitat, and from season to season, the basic pattern of carrion insect succession is remarkably constant around the world. Entomological science applied in a forensic context has the potential of serving as a valuable intelligence counter-deception tool which may help solve international crimes, to include war crimes against humanity in such places where genocide and mass grave movement have taken place (Kosovo, Iraq, etc.). This is accomplished by understanding the blowfly's life cycle, estimating PMI, and applying it to law or intelligence.

For example, a forensic entomologist can estimate PMI by examining the carrion insect population near the body. One can also estimate how long the deceased has been lying in a particular location by sampling the soil and insects underneath the deceased. If there is a difference in the estimates, and the analysis of the soil suggests a short PMI while the analysis of the body fauna suggests a longer PMI, one can determine that the body has been moved. One can also estimate how long the body has been lying at a certain place by analyzing the plants and the soil surrounding the body.[8] Other examples will be discussed later.

Insects in these cases tend to be "nature's intelligence agents"; they arrive on decomposing corpses in a relatively predictable sequence and in turn provide valuable scientific

---

[7] Wayne D. Lord and F. Berger, "Collection and Preservation of Forensically Important Entomological Materials," *Journal of Forensic Sciences* 28, (1983): 936-944.

[8] Starkeby, M., "Ultimate Guide to Forensic Entomology: Introduction to Forensic Entomology," Web-only essay, URL< http://folk.uio.no/mostarke/forens_ent/ introduction.html>, accessed 5 January 2004.

information. This is termed "ecological succession" and consists of a series of blending waves of different arthropods. Differences in the cast of carrion-frequenting insects (flies, beetles, spiders, ants, etc.) can be used to describe incidents surrounding the death. Some insects such as blowflies are the first to invade a corpse, while others such as dermestid beetles arrive later, removing the final bits of soft tissue. The time sequence in which carrion insects arrive, to include the season, provides investigators data to estimate the time of death, reveal movement of the body from one location to another (deception), or possibly detect explosive compounds utilized in a bombing. Information obtained from the insects is important because it can help the IC analyst or investigator determine what actions were taken by the perpetrator(s), reveal the time of the crime, and possibly reveal if explosives were utilized, to include possible type.

Upon identifying explosive materials/residues during chemical analysis, these can be compared in reference to materials believed to be utilized by certain individuals or factions. For example, larva samples from a previous bombing victim are submitted for chemical analysis and test positive for TNT. This sample can then be compared to an unknown sample of explosives recovered at another location (e.g., terrorist safehouse). If both samples reveal an identical chemical signature, one can ascertain the same explosive compounds were used by the same terrorist cell. This type of information becomes available only if the insects are properly collected and taken to a professional forensic entomologist for extraction and chemical analysis.

CONTRIBUTION TO THE INTELLIGENCE COMMUNITY

Utilization of forensic entomology can help analysts and others in a task force environment find the "ground truth" about what happened in cases of high-profile crimes. Its applicability could also help many other communities outside the U.S. IC, domestically and internationally—such as assisting EOD units; allied intelligence agencies (British MI5, MI6); local and state law enforcement (police departments, sheriffs); court systems and international tribunal courts (e.g., Sierra Leone, East Timor, Kosovo, Cambodia); and the North Atlantic Treaty Organization (NATO). The science as a whole would allow officers and analysts of these institutions to expand their evidence collection capability and help answer key questions involving war crimes and the deaths of civilian, military, and intelligence personnel.

The end product of finding such information could also be strategic in nature, with implications for sanctioning a nation that is not in compliance with the Geneva Conventions. The science is intended to help investigators reveal truth and put together cases against international leaders who practice criminal acts against innocent civilians. More importantly, it is intended to be utilized as a tool to fix individual accountability and help dispel the notion of collective guilt.

To achieve the end product discussed, one needs to understand forensic entomology. Studies reveal that carrion insects are generally the first to discover a corpse, particularly if any attempt has been made to hide the body. Often in outdoor death cases, blowflies (green, blue, or black bottle) will arrive and begin laying eggs on the body within minutes of the death. The gap between forensic entomology and intelligence can be filled by utilizing the fly's life cycle, thus estimating the time of death or PMI.

The theory behind estimating PMI with the help of insects is very simple: since insects arrive on the body soon after death—within 24 hours—estimating the age of the insect larvae will provide an estimation of the time of death.

As Haskell and Catts note, insects are important and often ignored or even discarded as evidence at a death scene or an autopsy. Western culture generally views maggots and flies as repulsive intruders to be avoided or destroyed. Unfortunately, this attitude is sometimes held also by death scene investigators and coroners. Conversely, even the absence of insects in situations where they should be present is valuable evidence in any investigation.[9]

In short, the American Board of Forensic Entomology (ABFE) holds that forensic entomology helps validate data and is considered another avenue for finding out the truth.[10] It is a tool which could enable law enforcement and intelligence officials to narrow the field of suspects, fix the time of death, reveal if bodies have been moved, and assist in identification of the deceased with reference to known missing persons.

The present study will reveal if explosive compounds can be extracted from blowfly larvae or pupae, thus revealing chemical composition. Upon identification of the chemical composition (chemical signature), the information can be used along with other identifiers to prove or disprove a hypothesis that the substance came from a certain manufacturer or locale. Such comparative explosive samples can also be obtained from clothing, footwear, and under fingernails, thus connecting the suspect to the crime. The items then can be compared to trace evidence or other articles in question. If analysis is conducted properly one can possibly reveal that the suspect came in contact with such specific substances; unquestionably, he or she could be tied to the crime that was committed. The information can then be applied to an intelligence product and disseminated to leading policymakers in the field who can take political or military action to interdict the supply of explosives at their source.

---

[9] Neal Haskell and N. Catts, *Entomology and Death: A Procedural Guide* (Clemson, South Carolina: Joyce's Print Shop, Inc., 1990), 2.

[10] Jason. H. Byrd, member of American Board of Forensic Entomology, interview by author, 28 March 2004.

KEY TERMS

Key terms are introduced here to give the reader a better understanding of some of the specialized language in the field. Other terms are explained in the Glossary.

ABFE: American Board of Forensic Entomology

AFME: Armed Forces Medical Examiner

ATF: Bureau of Alcohol, Tobacco, and Firearms

Calliphoraidae: The third suborder of Diptera which contains houseflies, bluebottles, greenbottles, and their relatives

DIA: Defense Intelligence Agency

Explosives: Substances that can explode, e.g., TNT

FBI: Federal Bureau of Investigation

Forensic Entomology: The study of insects and related arthropods from a medical/legal perspective

Green Bottle Blowfly: Part of the Diptera family; species of blowfly whose features include shiny metallic green back with hair on thorax and abdomen

Genocide: Systematic killing of an entire group of people

Homicide: Killing of a person by another

Medico-Legal Entomology: Medical use of entomology from a legal viewpoint

Metabolic: Changing of food by organisms into energy cells, etc.

Porcine: Pork meat or muscle

Postmortem Interval: The period of time between death and a corpse discovery

Suicide: Act of killing one's self intentionally

Violent Crimes: Crimes which exhibit great force, thus breaking the law

FORENSIC ENTOMOLOGY: A TOOL TO HELP SOLVE WAR CRIMES

The use of insect behavior to estimate the time of death is not a modern concept. The earliest recorded crime investigation with insects was in 1235 A.D. in China. Sung Tz'u, a Chinese "death investigator," wrote a book entitled *The Washing Away of Wrongs*. This medico-criminal entomology case was recounted as a murder by slashing, which occurred in a Chinese village, and the local death investigator was deputized to solve the crime. After some fruitless questioning, the investigator had all the villagers bring their sickles to one spot and lay them out before the crowd. Flies landed on only one of the sickle sticks. This was due to blood being spattered on the sickle. The owner subsequently broke down and confessed to the crime.[11]

In 1668 Redi studied rotting meat that was either exposed to or protected from flies. From his analysis of subsequent blowfly infestation, he refuted the hypothesis of the "spontaneous generation" of life. Up to that time it was generally believed that under the right conditions maggots came from rotten meat. Until the seventeenth century it was believed that the presence of "worms" (maggots) in corpses was due to spontaneous generation. Redi proved by his experiments that these larvae came from fly eggs deposited on putrefying carcasses.[12]

Later near Paris, France, Bergeret (1850) was the first Westerner to use insects as forensic indicators. The body of a baby was found behind the plaster mantle in a house, and an investigation was begun. Bergeret determined that the assemblage of insects associated with the corpse pointed to a state of decay that dated back several years; consequently, the question of guilt was thrown upon the earlier occupants of the house and not upon the current ones.[13]

More recently, a decade has passed since Serb execution squads shot, knifed, axed, and clubbed to death about 7,000 Muslims from the United Nations "safe area" of Srebrenica (in the former Yugoslavia). The media routinely billed these killings as Europe's largest mass murder since the Second World War. They were actually its largest since Tito's execution squads shot, knifed, axed, and clubbed to death about 35,000 Croats, Muslims, Slovenes, Serbs, White Russians, and Cossacks in the weeks after World War II had ended.

These crimes, separated by 50 years, a few hundred miles, and a universe of social, economic, and political changes, show how human depravity has remained constant

---

[11] K. Smith, *A Manual of Forensic Entomology* (New York: Cornell University Press, 1986), 20-23.

[12] J. Guiart, "Notices Biographiques II: Francisco Redi 1628-1698," *Archives De Parisitologie* 1 (1898): 420.

[13] Smith, 30.

through the years. They also show how far the governments of the Western alliance have come in terms of their willingness to bring the perpetrators of such crimes to justice, at least when the victims are located in Europe's poor southeastern corner.

The similarities in these mass murders are striking. Almost all of the victims were prisoners, defeated soldiers, or civilians. Some had taken part in atrocities. Some were wounded and dragged from hospitals. None had a trial. Many died with their hands bound with wire and their throats cut. The killers buried the bodies in mass graves.

USE OF FORENSIC ENTOMOLOGY IN WAR CRIMES

Forensic entomology, specifically medico-legal entomology, is the science of using insect life cycle data combined with other evidence to uncover circumstances of interest to domestic crimes, such as homicide, suicide, movement of bodies, drugging, and torture.[14] It is such techniques which can help the IC solve international criminal acts against humanity, to include war crimes or terrorist activities which involve beheadings after which bodies are discarded at unknown locations. When the body is found in a mass grave or a crime scene is investigated, insects can provide clues as to what happened. Time of death may be ascertained; many clues about the cause of death or events just prior to death can be based on insect behavior and interaction with a corpse. Often drugging and the location of death can be determined by analyzing species and the growth of a maggot. This can help intelligence analysts and law enforcement investigators ascertain whether death occurred at the scene, or if the body was moved at some point in time, important elements in any war crime investigation.

Insects have roamed the earth for 250 million years.[15] This enormous amount of time has allowed insects to attain a wide diversity in both form and behavior. Presently, there are about 700,000 described species and it is estimated there may be more than 10 million species of insects on earth.[16] Insects can prove useful if the information they provide is properly collected. Careful observation with knowledgeable expertise of faunal succession at a crime scene, added to known insect life cycle data, can lead the investigator to infer how long the victim has been available to insect activity (given that a set of circumstances has existed). The following medico-legal process reveals how these conclusions can be reached.

---

[14] Starkeby, "Ultimate Guide to Forensic Entomology: Introduction to Forensic Entomology," 2004.

[15] James L. Castner, "Ultimate Guide to Forensic Entomology: A Review of Forensic Identification Cards," Web-only essay, URL: <http://folk.uio.no/mostarke/forens_ent/reviewFIFC.html>, accessed 5 January 2004.

[16] Starkeby, "Ultimate Guide to Forensic Entomology: Introduction to Forensic Entomology," 2004.

MEDICO-LEGAL PROCESS

The medico-legal aspect of forensic entomology includes arthropod (spiders, insects) involvement in events such as murder, suicide, and rape, but also includes physical abuse and contraband trafficking (smuggling). The arthropod feature that is most important in medico-legal forensic entomology is the importance of carrion feeders; that is, they consume dead animals, including humans. Thus, they give valuable answers to important questions in any criminal investigation, such as whether death occurred at the recovery scene or the body was deceptively moved at some point in time following death.

After death, body temperature drops, rigor mortis sets in, and animal tissue, including that of humans, becomes attractive to a variety of insects and other invertebrates. Not surprisingly, flies, especially the Calliphoraidae (green bottle and blue bottle fly) larvae or maggots (Diptera), on which this study is primarily based, figure largely in the invasion of tissue. Usually females of the genus Calliphoraidae oviposit within minutes following death. Thus, the flies leave an evidence trail of egg batches, white to yellow and 2 mm in length, in the mouth, nose, ears, wounds and, if exposed, the anus and the genitalia within minutes of death.[17] These natural body openings provide moist, humid cavities, which enhance egg hatching and larval survival.

Although there are various methods of establishing time of death for a human corpse, such as histological, chemical, bacteriological, and zoological, the last approach is based on an entomological study of the cadaver and gives accurate results if the data are properly collected.

As Smith notes, the invertebrate fauna of carrion consists mostly of insects and, in its simplest form, the forensic explanation is based on the study of sequence with which green bottle blowfly or other fly species appear on the cadaver. The knowledge of the time required by each developmental stage at varying temperatures, and identification of species in all stages, allows for an estimate of time of death. It may also be possible to establish if the body has been moved or partly concealed during decomposition.[18]

After the first few hours of death, the green bottle blowfly deposits its eggs and the first instar phase begins. This process contains multiple stages of skin molting. Additional behavior patterns of restlessness, movement away from the body, and burrowing in soil also occur. Finally, a pupa (or puparium) is formed and metamorphosis into a sexually mature adult insect (Imago) occurs. The life cycle stages of the Calliphoraidae blowfly are as follows:

1. Egg	4. 3rd instar larvae or prepupa
2. 1st instar larva	5. Pupa (or puparium)
3. 2nd instar larva	6. Imago (sexually mature adult insect)

---

[17] Starkeby, "Ultimate Guide to Forensic Entomology: Introduction to Forensic Entomology," 2004.

[18] Smith, 20-23.

To better understand this development, see life cycle of the fly (Figure 1). Also, see timeline and stages of immature fly development (Figure 2).

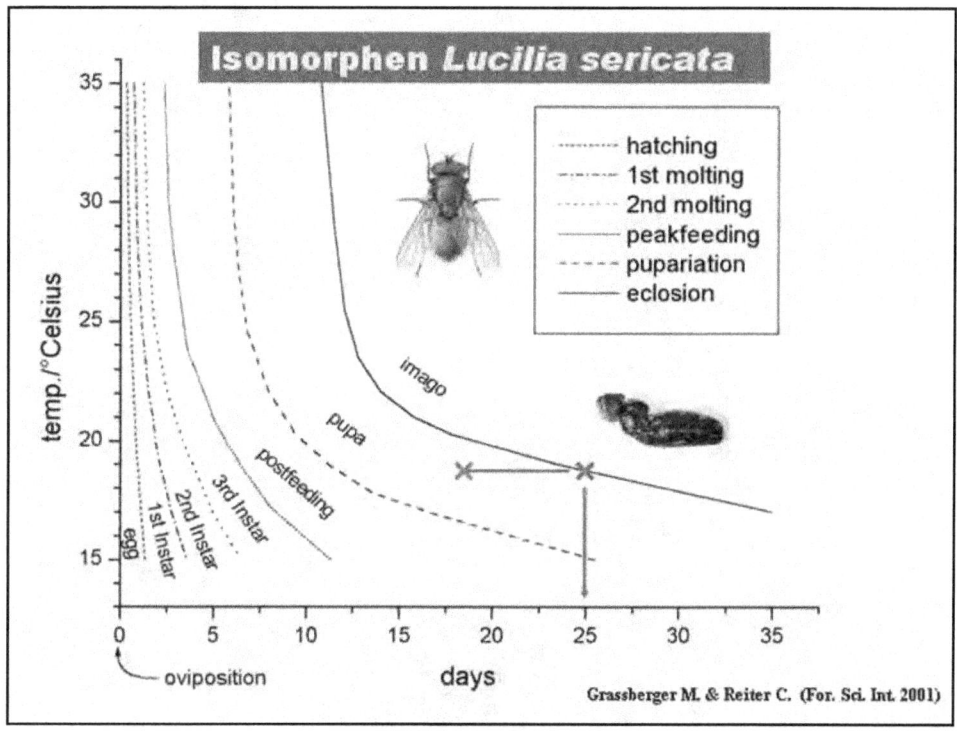

Figure 1. Fly Life Cycle

Source: M. Grassberger and C. Reiter, "Forensic Entomology: Post-Mortem Interval (PMI) Estimation Using Insect Development Data," *Institute of Forensic Medicine, University of Vienna,* URL: <http:// www.univie.ac.at/ forensic-entomology/ information.htm>, accessed 9 March 2004. Used with permission.

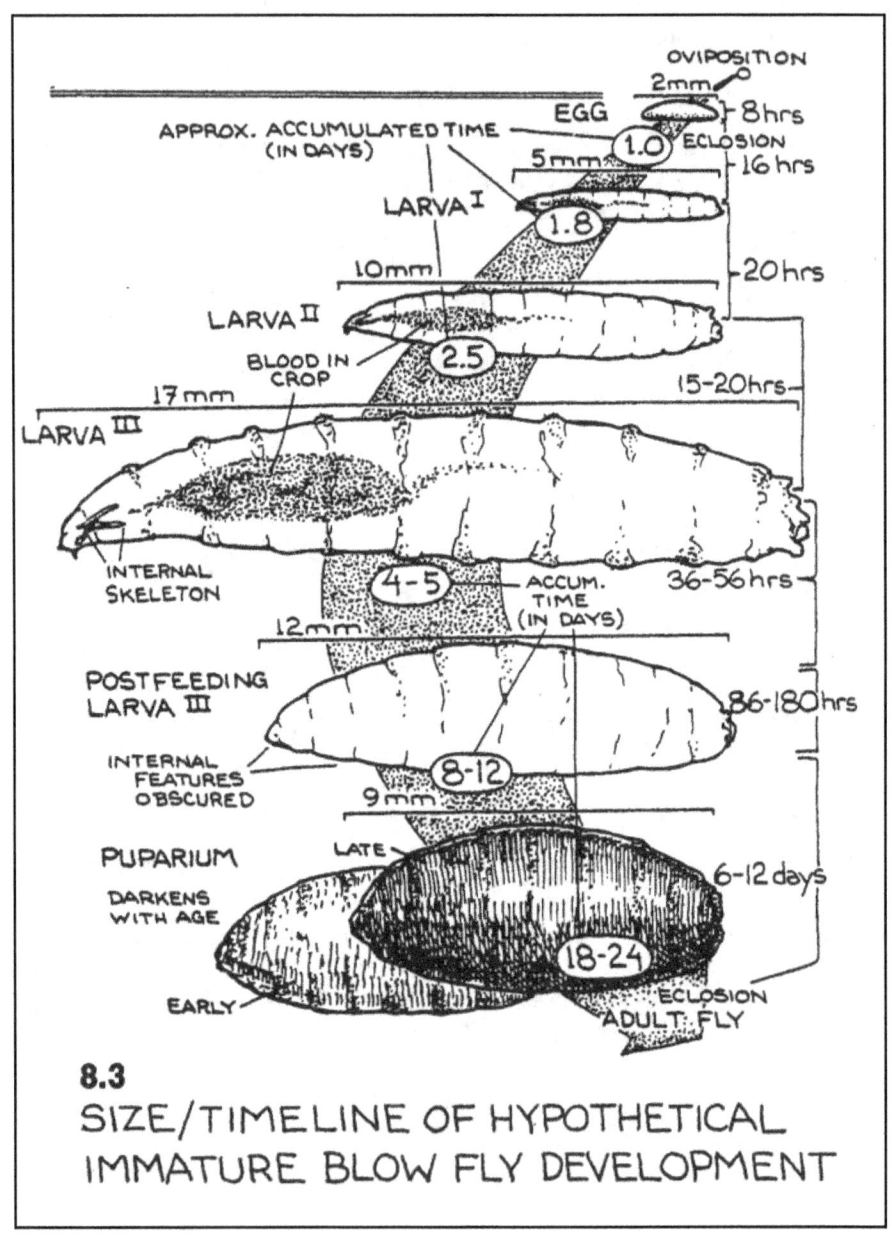

8.3 SIZE/TIMELINE OF HYPOTHETICAL IMMATURE BLOW FLY DEVELOPMENT

Figure 2. Timeline of Hypothetical Immature Blowfly Development

Source: Neal Haskell and N. Catts, *Entomology and Death: A Procedural Guide*, Clemson, SC: Joyce's Print Shop, 1990. Used with permission.

Note: Calliphoraidae (green bottle blowfly) and other fly genera lay eggs.[19] S. haemor-rhoidalis (red-tailed flesh fly) does not deposit eggs, only larvae.

The skill to accurately identify arthropods separates the forensic entomologist from other persons that are trained in evidence collection and evaluation. If one knows how long it takes to reach the different stages in an insect's life, one can calculate the age of the larva or deposition of eggs. This calculation of the insect age can be used to estimate a time of death or PMI in sun or shade, day or night.[20] Because of this, entomologists may be called upon to identify specimens for medico-legal purposes, and more importantly perhaps to confirm or invalidate a suspect's alibi in a murder case.

Can insects silently give us valuable information about a crime? The experts at the American Board of Forensic Entomology say we should be listening to insects through the evidence they provide us. Can they tell us when and where someone was murdered, or even possibly who did it? Can they tell us what type of explosive material was used in a bombing? This study and numerous green bottle blowflies may help us decide that we should be listening.

EVIDENTIARY APPROACH

Entomologists must collect, preserve, label, and ship insects or soil samples properly. Because there are various techniques in shipping, investigators should discuss handling techniques with their cooperating entomologist. Once proper techniques are established, a highly skilled entomologist can analyze the living or dead specimens in a laboratory facil-ity and determine the PMI or other vital information relating to a domestic or interna-tional investigation.

The analysis of entomological evidence can provide important information that may redirect a war crime investigation. Therefore, it is paramount that analysis and conclu-sions be as unbiased as possible. Entomological evidence is evaluated empirically, which means that the conclusions in an individual case are no more precise than the data they are based upon. This requires a review of how data were collected to determine if they are reliable enough for a domestic or international court of law.

The next few pages will cover many aspects of forensic entomology as practiced around the globe. Subdisciplines include faunal succession and cellular degradation; seasonality of certain insect fauna; estimation of the time of death; revealing deception by movement of body(ies) from one location to another (grave sites); PMI; death scene and the collecting of evidence, to include photographing, labeling, and transporting; finding the cause of death by analyzing drugs; significance of infestation of larvae and its significance to the IC; and lastly detection of drugs, chemical toxins, biological agents, and explosive compounds.

---

[19] H. Oldroyd, *Natural History of Flies* (New York: Norton Library, 1964), 110.

[20] Starkeby, "Ultimate Guide to Forensic Entomology: Introduction to Forensic Entomology," 2004.

FAUNAL SUCCESSION

When a person or animal dies, cells in the body immediately begin to break down and the body temperature changes to that of its surroundings, followed by rigor mortis (see Table 1). The temperature and stiffness of the postmortem body change after death as follows:

Temperature of body	Stiffness of body	Time since death
Warm →	Not stiff →	Not dead more than 3 hours
Warm →	Stiff →	Dead 3 to 8 hours
Cold →	Stiff →	Dead 8 to 36 hours
Cold →	Not stiff →	Dead more than 36 hours

Table 1. The Stages of Rigor Mortis

Source: Starkeby, "Ultimate Guide to Forensic Entomology: Introduction to Forensic Entomology."

During this series of events, postmortem putrefaction (decomposition of organic matter, production of foul-smelling matter) results in the release of gases, to which blowflies, flesh flies, and other carrion feeders are attracted.[21] The soft tissues of the deceased are generally destroyed quickly by the action of insects and their larvae. This degradational action occurs in a definite order, depending on the state of decomposition of the body.[22] When the body is discovered, the state of activity taking place can reveal a great deal of information about the death. This information is deduced by the processing of entomological evidence. Smith established an order of decay. Noting that various organs of the body decompose at different rates and may also be used to estimate the time of death, the usual order is:

1. Intestines, stomach, liver blood, heart blood and circulation, heart muscle
2. Air passage and lungs
3. Brain
4. Kidney and bladder
5. Voluntary muscles
6. Uterus

The putrefaction process results in the release of gases such as ammonia, hydrogen sulfide, carbon dioxide, and nitrogen.[23] During this stage the skin becomes greenish black and the body becomes bloated. The putrefaction process is largely due to microscopic organisms invading the body.[24]

---

[21] Starkeby, "Ultimate Guide to Forensic Entomology: Introduction to Forensic Entomology." 2004.

[22] B. Fisher, *Techniques of Crime Scene Investigation* (Boca Raton, FL: CRC Press, 1993), 72.

[23] Smith, 86.

[24] G. Bianchini, "La Biologia Del Cadaver," *Archivic Antropologia Criminale, Psichiatria e Medicina Legale* 50, (1930): 1035-1105.

Hobson found that initially the insect order Diptera (fly) appears after the onset of putrefaction, depending on the time of year and the situation of the corpse. The activities of this fly accelerate putrefaction and the disintegration of the corpse. Also, Hobson found that larvae feed on liquid between the muscle fibers because the tissues are too acidic. Later, when tissue becomes alkaline, the intermuscular tissue is attacked.[25]

This has a relevance to entomologists' investigations since some of the experimental field work on carrion insect fauna has been conducted with waves of infestation or succession. Different workers have interpreted these waves of insects during the succession of carrion. Nevertheless, the existence of a successional pattern is recognizable.

SEASONALITY

Seasonality can also play an important role when estimating the time of death on a cadaver. Some insects, such as June beetles, are seasonal and appear only for a few months out of the year, usually during spring to winter. This factor can help analysts and investigators narrow the timeline. Bornemissza established that the original fauna plays a minor part in decomposition and that the rate of decay will vary with temperature, season, microclimate, and other environmental factors. Species lists will differ regionally and also determine whether the corpse initially was in a lit or shaded area.[26] Vertebrate scavengers may play a larger role in the tropics. Nevertheless, careful collection of data on site, coupled with biological knowledge of the insects concerned, will enable a reconstruction of events including an estimated time of death.

In temperate regions dead bodies are often located in the spring, after the snow has melted. The forensic entomologist and the forensic pathologist must then try to determine whether the death occurred during the winter or before the snow set in. If the death occurred before November in the northern hemisphere, it is possible to find dead insects in and on the body. This is accomplished by analyzing the dead insect fauna, and determining when the insects probably died (this can be found by looking at meteorological records). Another hint is when the different adults stop flying before the winter. For example, in Norway, where bodies have been found in the spring, in one case a dead 3rd stage blowfly larva was found in the back of the mouth. The blowfly larva was of a species that is present from May to October. It was concluded from this examination that the eggs were probably laid during October and, since there were relatively few larvae, probably late in October. In another case, several living insects and many dead 3rd instar larvae were found on a dead body. The dead larvae were found on the stomach, the arms, the shoulders, and inside the head. Investigators in this case concluded that the live insects had colonized the dead body in the spring, and that the larvae had died during the winter.[27]

---

[25] P. Hobson, "Studies of the Nutrition of Blowfly Larvae, III: The Liquefaction of Muscle." *Journal of Experimental Biology* 9, (1932): 359-365.

[26] F. Bornemissza, "An Analysis of Arthropod Succession in Carrion and the Effect of its Decomposition on the Soil Fauna," *Australian Journal of Zoology* 5 (1957): 1-12.

[27] Haskell and Catts, 11.

Another insect that can be utilized in cases which cover the spring to summer months is the green June beetle. It is known that only one generation of adults matures each year. Grubs over-winter up to a foot (0.3 m) or more below the soil surface. Green June beetles gradually make their way close to the surface during the spring, and feed mainly on decaying plant matter and to a lesser degree on roots. [28] Biological knowledge of the insects concerned will enable a reconstruction of events including an estimated time of death.

POSTMORTEM INTERVAL (PMI): ESTIMATING THE TIME OF DEATH

The theory behind estimating time of death, or PMI, with the help of insects is very simple: since insects arrive on the body soon after death, estimating the age of the insects will also lead to an estimation of the time of death. The stages of development in the Calliphoraidae blowfly are helpful in this regard (see Figure 2).

A more precise way to determine age of larvae and eggs is the use of rearing. For example, the body is found with masses of eggs on it, or none has hatched. How long is it since the eggs were oviposited (laid)? Note the time of the discovery; note the time when the 1st instar larvae occurred. Subtract the first occurrence time from the discovery time (call this time A). Rear the blowflies to adults and let them lay eggs on raw beef liver under conditions similar to the crime scene, and take the time from oviposition to the first occurrence of 1st instar larvae (call this time B). By calculating B minus A, one gets C, which is an estimate of the time from oviposition to discovery. Similar calculations can be made for other instars as well. If one has good baseline data from before under different temperatures and for different species, one only needs to rear the flies to a stage where they can be identified, that is, the 3rd instar stage of the adult stage.

M. Chang and W. Rodriguez note that certain crawling insects are highly predictable, especially blowflies of the family Calliphoraidae.[29] Typically, these flies detect the cadaver's odor of decay and lay eggs on or near fresh corpses soon after death. Thus, the maggots' developmental clock can provide an accurate measure of the body's PMI, a variable that is of interest to investigators.[30]

Bornemissza recognizes that the carrion community has four ecological categories. Some species simply seek moisture while others require a place to rest and feed on both the corpse and its inhabitants.[31] The four categories of the carrion community are as follows:

---

[28] Bill Hilton, Jr., Hilton Pond Center, "June Bug's Gotta Eat Too," Web-only essay, 8-14 July 2002, URL: <www.http://images.searches.yahoo.com>, key work June beetle, accessed 27 May 2004.

[29] M. Chang, "Fly Witness," *Science World Journal* 54, no. 4 (1997): 8.

[30] William Rodriguez, Ph.D., DoD Coroner, Washington, DC. Interview by the author, 16 December 2003.

[31] Bornemissza, 5-12.

1. Necrophagous species—Feed on the carrion itself and constitute the most important category in establishing time of death. Diptera: Calliphoraidae (blowflies); Sarcophaga haemorrhoidalis (red-tailed flesh fly); Coleoptera: Staphylinidae (rove-beetles) specialize on bone.

2. Predators and parasites on the necrophagous species—Second most important forensic category. Coleoptera: Silphidae (in part); Staphylinidae; Diptera: some carrion feeders become predaceous in later instars (eat larvae).

3. Omnivorous species—Wasps, ants and some Coleoptera: Staphylinidae (rove-beetles) feed on both the corpse and its inhabitants (larvae).

4. Adventive species—Use the corpse as an extension of their environment. Collembola: Isotoma sepulchralis (springtails); spiders (which may become incidental predators).

The insects that usually arrive first at a death scene are the Diptera, in particular the Calliphoridae (blowfly) and Sarcophagidae (flesh fly). Beetles and wasps soon follow to devour rotting flesh, dried skin, and hair. The difference between the two flies is that Sarcophagidae give birth to live larvae, due to their ability to hatch eggs in the uterus instead of laying eggs.[32] After a short time, depending on species, the females of Calliphordae lay their eggs or larvae within one to two days on natural orifices of the body, especially the eyes, nose, ears, anus, and the genital areas.[33, 34] Wounds also provide another easy access point, with blood as a further attractant.[35]

The key to estimating PMI is based on how the insects develop under varying environmental conditions. After a short amount of time, depending on the species and the temperature, the egg hatches into a small larva. As noted before, the larva measures about 2 mm in length and lives off decaying tissue, growing at a rapid rate. After two days of feeding, the larva molts to the 2nd instar, gaining 2-3 mm in length. The larva continues to feed, reaching 3rd instar in 4-5 days. By this stage, the maggot is about 17 mm long and restless. It migrates away from the corpse, seeking a suitable place to burrow itself into the ground and pupate, ending its prepupal stage. Prior to forming the puparium, the larva becomes less active and contracts its body into a shorter, thicker form, which becomes the puparium. This complete metamorphosis to adulthood typically takes a week to two weeks depending on the species of insect and the temperature in the surrounding area (see Figure 4). The rule of growth is the higher the temperature the faster the growth, whereas the lower the temperature the slower the rate of growth.

Figure 3 portrays the timeline associated with a corpse's decomposition, with a parallel timeline moving backward to estimate the time of death through faunal evidence.

---

[32] Oldroyd, 112.

[33] J. Sachs, "A Maggot for the Prosecution," *Discovery* 11 (1998): 103-108.

[34] Smith, 88.

[35] A. Gail and J. Gaudet, "A Practical Exercise in Forensic Entomology," *RCMP Gazette* 53, no. 11 (1999): 10-12.

As indicated in the figure, the postmortem interval, which is the period of time between death and discovery of the corpse, can be estimated fairly accurately, within a window of certainty bounded by maximal and minimal times.

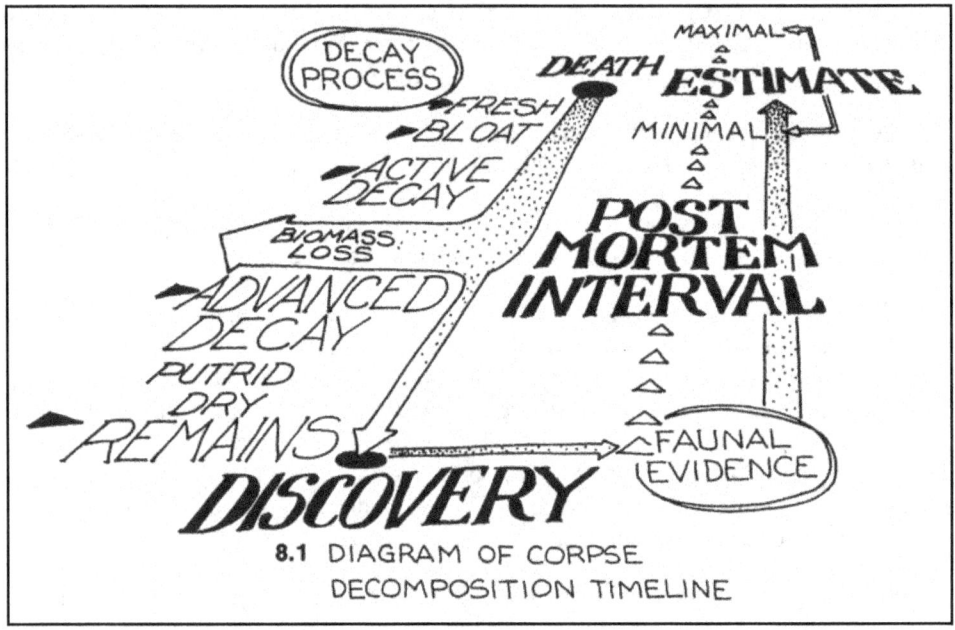

Figure 3. Decomposition Timeline

Source: Neal Haskell and N. Catta. *Entomology and Death: A Procedural Guide.* Clemson, SC: Joyce's Print Shop, 1990. Used with permission.

If sufficient information exists, the entomologist can establish a reasonable estimate of the minimum and maximum time the body was available to insects, to include an estimate in hours. For example, a coroner retrieves a newly formed pupa of a particular fly from a death scene (e.g., Kosovo). The entomologist knows that this particular fly could arrive at this location within an hour of death and that the eggs of this fly take an average of 400 hours (390 to 410) to pupate at the temperature of the corpse. The entomologist then calculates by adding one hour, estimating the PMI near 401 hours, but no lower than 391 hours and no greater than 411 hours (if the temperature of the crime scene was constant this would simplify the calculations of PMI).

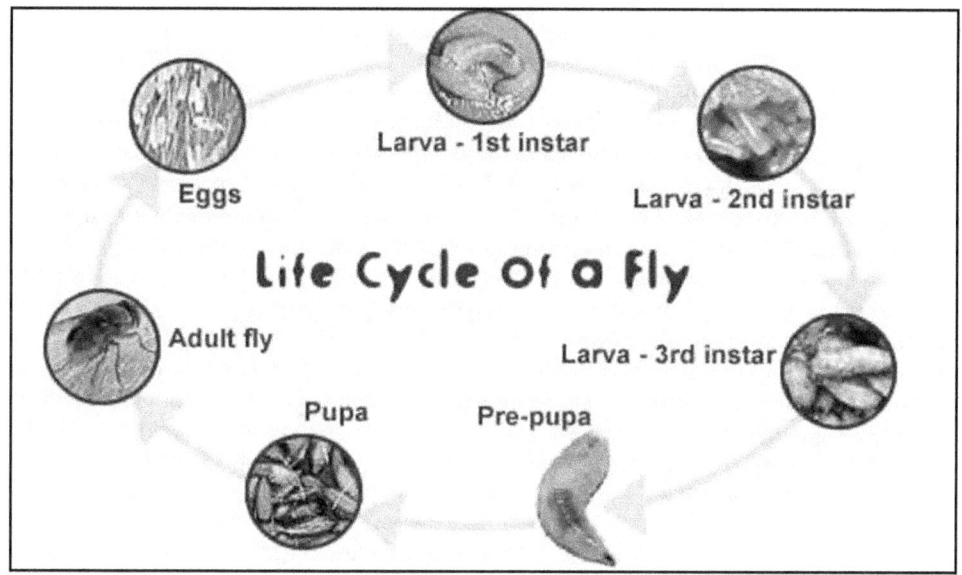

Figure 4. Fly Life Cycle

Source: "Decomposition: What Happens to the Body After Death?" *Australian Museum,* 2003, URL:<http://images.search.yahoo.com/search/images/view, accessed 9 March 2004. Used with permission.

However, if a body has been exposed to the environment for a longer period of time, flies may have gone through multiple life cycles. Therefore, the presence of other insects from subsequent successional waves will be useful in providing an estimate of the date of death.

In addition to estimating the time of death, insects can provide the analyst with the ability to find ground truth, in this case, the deceptive movement of a body or bodies that are in question at a scene, to include answers as to what happened to a body in a shallow grave. The following case studies are provided for illumination.

COLLECTION OF EVIDENCE

Within the United States and in other countries around the globe, insect scientists (entomologists) are being utilized with increasing frequency to apply their knowledge and expertise to criminal and civil case proceedings, and to become recognized members of forensic laboratories and medical/legal investigation teams. Such forensic facilities are nationwide and are considered highly specialized laboratories that provide forensic examiners and law enforcement personnel with the appropriate tools to support criminal investigations. In addition to supporting law enforcement criminal investigations, these laboratories could be used to assist in fighting the global war on terrorism by gathering hard evidence to prosecute those who commit heinous crimes against humanity.

In a report disseminated 8 October 2003 by the U.S. Department of Justice, Federal Bureau of Investigation Director Robert S. Mueller III described how important forensic laboratories were to the IC: "Regional Forensic Laboratories play an important role in the fight against terrorism by providing critical and timely forensic expertise. Additionally, our examiners have helped secure convictions … against murderers. This program is a smart solution that is positively impacting the way we address complex crimes."[36]

THE SIGNIFICANCE OF BLOWFLIES

Because blowfly biology varies among species, and with different environmental conditions, the following information is general. The black blowfly differs from the green and blue bottle blowflies in that it is a cool weather insect which overwinters in the adult stage and is most numerous in early spring or autumn. The green and blue bottle blowflies are abundant during the warm, humid summer months and over-winter as larvae or pupae.

A case in which blowflies were of great importance involved a murder crime where a victim was thrown down an open well on a farm located in a rural area in central Indiana.[37] The exact location of the remains was unknown to investigators. During the investigation, a search was conducted at several wooded farmyard well sites—the area where the body was presumed to have been. Haskell and Catts note that the correct site was obvious due to several thousand flies hovering over the debris of tires and rocks that were in the well obstructing the body. Upon recovering the corpse, investigators noted the body was in an advanced decay stage, with no insects found on it. They concluded that access to the body by blowflies was restricted by the materials. The odor is the contributing factor here that attracted the multitude of insects and led investigators to find the body.

The information gained from this case study can be applied to mass grave burials. In cases such as genocide and mass grave burials in Kosovo, intelligence utilized overhead satellites and visual imagery—to provide policymakers with answers as to the possibility of mass burials. Images led investigators and analysts to conclude that soil had been moved or tilled (e.g., ditches and plots).

However, satellites do not have the ability to reveal the whole truth—in this case, revealing if bodies had been buried at the gravesite shown by imagery. By applying forensic entomology science, however, ground teams can obtain viable evidence, estimate the time of death of the bodies, and confirm that bodies are buried at the gravesite shown by the satellite's visual images. In addition, this counter-deception and unconventional inves-

---

[36] U.S. Department of Justice, Federal Bureau of Investigation, *"FBI Director Mueller Announces Five New Computer Forensic Laboratories,"* Washington, DC: FBI National Press Office, 8 October 2003, URL: <http://www.fbi.gov/pressrel/pressrel03/lab100803.htm>, accessed 9 June 2004.

[37] Haskell and Catts, 11-12.

tigative technique, utilizing insects, can provide intelligence analysts with valuable answers as to where a body or bodies might have been moved. Insects hovering over a suspected gravesite provide evidence of the possibility of a buried body or bodies, much like buzzards do when carcasses are present in the desert.

REVEALING DENIAL AND DECEPTION:
MOVEMENT OF THE BODY

Insect evidence may provide clues as to whether a body was disturbed or moved after death. Roy Godson and James Wirtz, authors of *Strategic Denial and Deception: The 21st Century Challenge*, define denial as "the attempt to block information that could be used by an opponent to learn some truth, and deception as the ability to mask or confuse an opponent through disguise."[38] Denial and deception occur when one tries to mask some piece of information, such as information about an event, from being discovered to gain time or leverage. An example of denial is Serbian soldiers killing innocent Albanians, then placing the bodies in mass graves, thus preventing inspectors from discovering the crime of ethnic cleansing and genocide.

A murder victim transported to another location may show signs consistent only with the original location. When dealing with entomology, different species have different habitat preferences and are also seasonal. For example, one species of green bottle fly, Lucilia sericata, prefers well-lit areas when breeding, while the black blowfly (Phormia regina) prefers shade.[39] When investigators found black blowflies on the rotting body of a woman in a Maryland landfill, they became suspicious. Her remains, discovered in July 1984, lay in an area often exposed to direct sunlight and frequented by green bottle flies. Since no green bottle flies were found on her body, investigators concluded that she had been moved from a more shaded environment preferred by black blowflies. Investigators used this and other evidence to track down the killer.[40]

Morten Staerkeby gives insight to another case in Azerbaijan, dated 5 May 1962. He describes a body found, partly skeletonized and badly decomposed, in a saltwater tank used for firefighting. He adds, "Laboratory experiments on live fly larvae found on the body and trousers showed that they could not survive in saltwater, thus proving that the body had been in the tank for only a short time. Obviously, the death had occurred at another site and the body had been moved. Based upon examination of the larvae it was estimated that the death had occurred some seven to ten days earlier. Confession of the killer confirmed that the victim was shot on 26 April 1962 (nine days earlier than the discovery of the body) and

---

[38] Roy Godson and James J. Wirtz, "Strategic Denial and Deception," in *Strategic Denial and Deception: The 21st Century Challenge* (New Brunswick, NJ: Transaction Publications, 1997), 1.

[39] May R. Barenbaum, *Ninety-Nine More Maggots, Mites, and Munchers* (Urbana and Chicago: University of Illinois Press, 1985), 10-46.

[40] Gail and Gaudet, 12-14.

the body was placed in the tank on 4 May 1962. In addition, a fly pupa related to those on the body was found on the seat of the car used to transport the corpse."[41]

Cases which have been solved by forensic entomology can be applied to military action internationally. Serbian forces on 24 April 1999 were accused of committing atrocities, killing and burying innocent civilians in mass graves in the villages of Pusto Selo and Izbica, Kosovo. In the article, Agence France Presse argues that NATO's aerial photos of mass graves, taken by satellite, were fabricated. NATO showed two photographs using comparative analysis of each village. [42]

In each case, one of the photos shows the area before the alleged graves were dug and the second, taken several days later, appears to show a number of freshly dug graves.[43] To counter such a claim, counter-deception using forensic entomology should be applied to find the truth. Allied teams of state and federal investigators, to include forensic anthropologists, odontologists, and entomologists could be put on the ground to reveal if graves were dug recently and if the bodies were in fact buried in the area described by the satellite photos. Here, forensic anthropologists could reveal the cause of death, explaining whether trauma had been directed to a certain location on a body by a specific weapon. Forensic odontology can reveal the identification of a body through dental analysis. And forensic entomology could reveal time of death by rearing and evaluating the growth of the insect that had infested the corpse, as well as reveal if deceptive movement had occurred, as in the domestic cases with the black and green blowflies.

The cases discussed can be applied to the theory of tracking and revealing deceptive operations, such as the movement of bodies from one gravesite to another. Forensic entomology thus sheds light on the criminal act that is being hidden by a specific person or force which is or was in-country during a specific time and at a specific place. This concept is a valuable tool for denial and deception practitioners, specifically because it can be used as a counter-deception tool to determine "ground truth."

Another way of looking at defeating an adversary who has hidden a body or bodies at an unmarked location is by viewing insect behavior. In such a setting a fly would be able to defeat the well-developed camouflage of topsoil made by the adversary. The fly in this case would be able to smell small amounts of putrefaction of a corpse. The blowfly's sensory medium would cause the flies to hover over the unknown gravesite. An analyst just has to know the fly species in the region, to include breeding and eating habits, then seek out mass hovering to identify the location where a body or bodies may have been laid or deposited. In short, the fly's keen olfaction enhances the investigator's visual acuity; find-

---

[41] Starkeby, "Ultimate Guide to Forensic Entomology: Introduction to Forensic Entomology."

[42] Brent Sadler and others, "NATO: Aerial Photo May Show Mass Graves in Kosovo," *CNN,* online ed., 11 April 1999, URL:<http://www.cnn.com/WORLD/ europe/9904/11/nato.attack.05/>, accessed 1 June 2004.

[43] Emperor's Clothes, "Were NATO's Aerial Photo's of Mass Graves Faked?" Web-only essay, Spring and Fall, URL: <http://emperor.vwh.net/misc/graves2.htm.>, accessed 1 June 2004.

ing flies finds graves. Such information could reveal one location or multiple ones, thus having the potential to identify clandestine movement.

Nonetheless, the application of carrion insects to crime is only as good as the people who recognize it and accept the science as a tool. In short, it is a science which can be applied in any environment, even a military operation at sea.

Such an operation, which was put into play at sea in 1943, was the deceptive invasion of Sicily, known as Operation MINCEMEAT. British counterintelligence agent Ewen Montagu explains in his book *The Man Who Never Was* how Operation MINCEMEAT called for the use of a dead body, with a made-up identity, dressed as a Royal Marine officer and presumably killed in an airplane crash, to wash ashore near the town of a known Nazi agent of Spain. The deception would include dated theater tickets, false identification card, and a deceptive letter discussing the assault. All information would be planted on the body. The operation was designed to hide the true intention of the real invasion of Sicily in June 1943.[44] Historically, the operation was a complete success. Nonetheless, one must take a look from a counter-deception standpoint and utilize Analysis of Competing Hypotheses (ACH) to reveal if the deception could have been compromised.

Hypothetically and from a counter-deception perspective, if the body had contained traces of insect infestation, 3rd instar blowfly larvae for example, the Germans might have estimated the time of death prior to the theater ticket stub dates. A list of observables follows:

1. 22 April 1943, theater tickets dated
2. 27 April 1943, aircraft is suspected of crashing and is the date of death...Medical Examiner in Madrid
3. 30 April 1943, body (Major Martin) was launched to shore by submarine
4. 30 April 1943, body was found by fisherman off shore of Huelva
5. 30 April 1943, body seen by Medical Examiner
6. 30 April 1943, body buried with full military funeral
7. 3 May 1943, British received a message from Naval Attaché in Madrid
8. Note one. Body is decomposed and in black putrefaction stage (12-20 days)
9. Note two. No bruises on body (aircraft crash)
10. Note three. 3rd instar at 70 degrees (11 days)

If the body had been found with 3rd stage instars or larvae it would have revealed that the body had made contact with flies on land. This would produce an estimate that the body's death or PMI is at 11 days. The deception plan puts the body in the water, to include being found by a fisherman on 30 April 1943 (30-11=19). The following numbers would suggest the time of death of Major Martin on 19 April 1943. In addition, the 19 April 1943 date would prove the theory that the theater tickets dated 22 April were planted. Second analysis reveals that the black putrefaction stage would have coincided with the 3rd instar

---

[44] Ewan Montagu, *The Man Who Never Was: World War II's Boldest Counterintelligence Operation* (Annapolis, MD: Naval Institute Press, 1996), 88-116.

stage. By viewing the photo and estimating the black putrefaction stage in which the body was found, death could be estimated to have occurred 11-12 days ago (30-12=18). The calculation would place the time of death at 18 April 1943. By comparing both dates, 18 and 19 April (3rd instar and putrefaction), it is clear that the dates are closer to each other, producing an estimate of the time of death between 18 and 19 April 1943.

In this case, ACH is helpful in countering such a deception, but only if the investigator or analyst is also in tune with the science of forensic entomology and its sub-disciplines. To better understand ACH an analyst should list all the observables in order, and evaluate the observables compared to the hypothesis using "C" for consistent and "I" for inconsistent. Then the analyst should eliminate non-diagnostic observables and apply a qualitative test using "+" or "-" to each observable. Upon completing the aforementioned, the analyst should eliminate the weak hypothesis, make a last sanity check with two other analysts, and add his own assumptions to determine the most strongly supported hypothesis. If followed correctly the results can lead the analyst to find "ground truth" with a high probability of success.

In closing, it is this type of scenario that can be utilized and applied to intelligence counter-deception and denial practices to include those in an international tribunal involving war crimes or in an International Criminal Court (ICC).

Although the exact species may differ from country to country, from habitat to habitat, and from season to season, the basic pattern of insect succession is remarkably consistent around the world. While a broad range of insect species are attracted to decomposing remains and play an active role in the decay process, two groups, flies (Diptera) and beetles (Coleoptera), are of major importance in most circumstances. Flies, specifically blowflies, are considered the first wave of insects to be attracted to, and to colonize, a decomposing corpse. Fly larvae quickly consume the corpse's skin, remaining soft tissue, and organs. Only much later, when the corpse is decomposed and reaching dry decay stage, does the second wave of insect species, notably beetles, appear, move in, and continue the process.

DEATH SCENE PROCEDURES

The overall success of forensic entomology with PMI begins with the death scene. A death scene is described as the location where the body was discovered. This is where the majority of insect evidence is collected. Collection of this material is always one of the most important tasks. Items must first be recognized as potential evidence, then collected properly to yield any forensic information.

Most of the evidence used in forensic entomology as discussed by Haskell and Catts is classified as "disappearing evidence," i.e., evidence that crawls, burrows, or takes flight in its surroundings. Therefore, it is important to learn the key habits of insects that surround the death scene so that proper collection and identification can be accomplished.[45] If doubt exists, the help of an expert entomologist should be sought to reduce errors. The expert will know the group as a whole and not just the narrow confines of normal forensic

---

[45] Haskell and Catts, 84.

application, which is vital in any case.[46] After consulting with an expert, one should examine the death scene carefully by making notes about the insects found in a particular ecosystem, keeping in mind proper scientific names.

To make the most of entomological evidence at a domestic or international war crime scene, an experienced and well-trained forensic entomologist should do the collecting. The exact procedure at the crime scene varies with the type of habitat and the time of year, but in general we can divide the work of the forensic entomologist into six parts:

1. Collection of specimens from the body before body removal.
2. Collection of specimens from the surrounding area (up to 6 m from the body) before removal of the remains.
3. Collection of specimens from directly under and in close proximity to the remains after the body has been removed.[47]
4. Visual observation and notations at the scene. Entomological evidence field notes are recommended.
5. Initiation of climatological data collection at the scene.
6. Shipping insects if needed.[48]

While at the death scene, and prior to the body's removal, any insect that is hovering around or settled on or under a corpse should be captured with a suitable net, transferred to a glass or plastic tube, killed, and preserved in 70 percent EtOH (Ethyl alcohol) or 70 percent Isopropyl alcohol for later study.[49] Other adult invertebrates that cannot fly should be placed into tubes with the aid of forceps, sticks, or grass stems. If kept alive, each specimen should be kept in a separate tube to avoid possible predation. Dadour and Cook give vivid detail of how evidence can consume evidence by noting that hairy maggots of genus Chrysomya are predaceous (taking prey) on other fly species and their own species if placed together.[50]

It is important to note the precise site and situation on the body where each sample is collected, and this should be recorded on the spot. The first insects to be collected are the adult flies and beetles. These insects are fast-moving and can leave the crime scene rapidly once disturbed. Eggs, maggots, and other larvae of all sizes feeding on the body should be removed from natural openings, including under and in folds of clothes. Collection of specimens should extend out to six meters of the body, should be handled with forceps, and again be placed into 70 percent alcohol or 70 percent Isopropyl alcohol and labeled (see Figure 5).

---

[46] Smith, 89.

[47] Starkeby, "Ultimate Guide to Forensic Entomology: Introduction to Forensic Entomology," 2004.

[48] Haskell and Catts, 90-96.

[49] Rodriguez interview.

[50] Dadour, I., and D. Cook, "Forensic Entomology," web-only essay, URL: <http:// www.agric.wa.gov.au:7000/ento/forensic.htm>, accessed 5 January 2004.

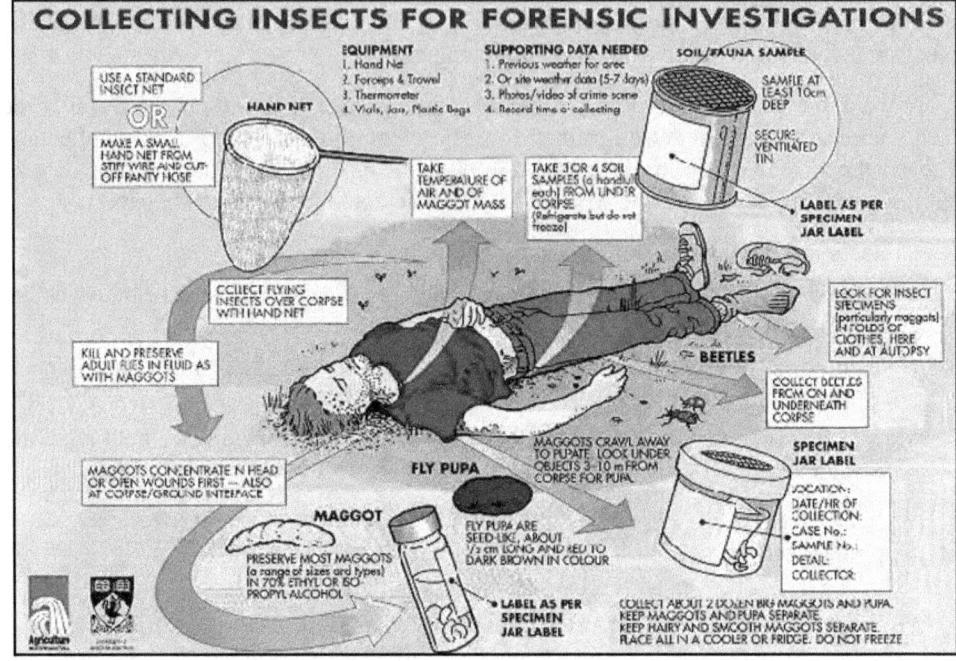

Figure 5. Collection Chart for Forensic Investigations

Source: Neal Haskell and Paul Catts, *Entomology and Death: A Procedural Guide*, Clemson, SC: Joyce's Print Shop, 1990. Used with permission.

Labeling

Container labels should indicate date and time the insects were collected, for example "5 May 2004, 0700 hours," geographical location, case number, location on the body where removed, name and agency of collector, and telephone number. Labels must be printed legibly using waterproof ink or pencil. An alternative method is using a dark pencil lead on bond paper with at least 50 percent rag content. Properly marked labels can then be placed in the container with the insect.[51]

Photos and the Recording of Climate Data

Following labeling, a full description of the site and condition of the corpse should be recorded, both with a diagram and 35 mm or digital photographs. An object such as a ruler or measuring tape should be used to identify overall length of maggots, pupae, position of the carcass, and inflicted wounds when photographing, if any.[52] Where possible, both a preserved and a living sample should be taken.[53] Physical conditions including

---

[51] Stephen Bullington, "Forensic Entomology," Web-only essay, 24 July 2001, URL: <http://www.key-net.net/users/swb/forensics>, accessed 5 January 2004.

[52] Rodriguez interview.

temperature, humidity, and precipitation, along with soil samples, should be gathered and recorded at the death scene (see Appendix A).

Collection of Climatological Data at the Scene

Such data should include:
1. Ambient air temperature at the scene taken approximately at chest height with the thermometer in the shade, and not exposing the thermometer to direct sunlight.
2. Maggot mass temperature. Obtained by placing thermometer directly into the larval mass.
3. Ground surface temperature.
4. Temperature at the interface of the body and ground. This is accomplished by
5. Temperature of the soil directly under the body. Taken immediately after body removal.placing thermometer between the two surfaces, ground and victim.
6. Weather data, including precipitation for a period of one-two weeks before the victim was last seen to three-five days after the body was recovered.

Most importantly, temperature must be considered in PMI calculations for its effects on rates of larval growth. Hall suggests that criminologists and intelligence officers must not only consider ambient temperature, but also temperature changes induced by the larvae themselves when they present themselves in high enough densities. In addition, the mass of larvae makes the temperature higher and accelerates instar to pupa development.[54]

If temperatures cannot be recorded on site, then one should locate the closest meteorological station or, if near a beach, a lifeguard station where records of high and low temperatures can be obtained.[55]

Transporting Entomological Evidence

Once flies have been collected and preserved, duplicate material should be made for rearing. Specimens can be placed into a specimen container, plastic cup, or aluminum foil rearing pouch with liver, a moist paper towel, and sealed with a form-fitting lid. Tiny holes should be made through the lid using a sewing needle for ventilation, or a screen vent may be used as an alternative (see Figure 6). Cups should be placed into a slightly larger container with newspaper to reduce jarring.[56] Mark the exterior of the container "live specimens" and package it for immediate shipping to a forensic entomologist using the U.S. Postal Service, the United Parcel Service (UPS), or other overnight delivery service.[57]

---

[53] Starkeby, "Ultimate Guide to Forensic Entomology: Introduction to Forensic Entomology," 2004.

[54] G. Hall, *The Blowflies of North America* (Baltimore, MD: Say, 1948), 58.

[55] Castner, "Ultimate Guide to Forensic Entomology: A Review of Forensic Identification Cards," 2004.

[56] Bullington, "Forensic Entomology," 2001.

[57] Castner, "Ultimate Guide to Forensic Entomology: A Review of Forensic Identification Cards," 2004.

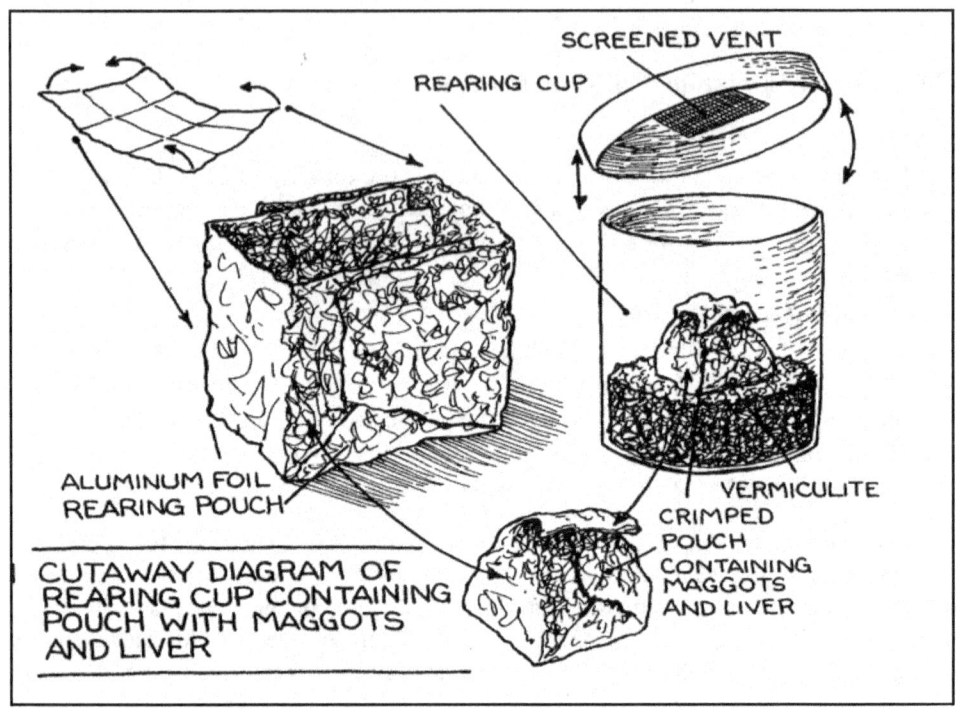

Figure 6. Packaging and Shipping of Live Specimens to a Forensic Entomological Laboratory

Source: Neal Haskell and N. Catts, Entomology and Death: A Procedural Guide, Clemson, SC: Joyce's Print Shop, 1990. Used with permission.

FINDING THE CAUSE
OF DEATH

In a lab, investigators can piece together where and when the victim died. Forensics has made it possible to use DNA technology not only to help determine insect species but to recover and identify the blood meals taken by blood-feeding insects. The DNA of human blood can be recovered from the digestive tract of an insect that has fed on an individual. The presence of the individual's DNA within the insect can place a suspect at a known location within a definable period of time. Recovery of the victim's blood can also create a link between perpetrator and suspect.[58] It is this theory which applies to the finding of explosive residues or compounds within the maggot's digestive tract or stored body fat content. However, instead of a DNA analysis, a chemical analysis is needed to ascer-

[58] Jason. H. Byrd, "Forensic Entomology: Insects in Legal Investigations," Web-only essay, URL: <http://www.forensic-entomology.com>, accessed 5 January 2004.

tain explosive chemical compound usage at a scene. The results of an explosive theory experiment will be provided in a subsequent section.

The sites of fly infestation on the corpse may also be important in determining the cause of death, or reconstruction of events prior to death. For example, if there has been trauma or mutilation of the body prior to death, this may lead to heavier infestation than with the limited natural openings. In knife and gunshot attacks, the use of the arms is common while protecting the face and head, resulting in injury to the lower part of the forearm. After death, these wounds are a breeding ground for flies.[59] Therefore, the natural behavior of oviposition or fly larva deposit on wounds can lead investigators to assume that self-defense was a factor and that homicide (murder) may have been the cause of death during a war crime.

DETECTION OF DRUGS, CHEMICAL TOXINS, BIOLOGICAL AGENTS, AND EXPLOSIVE COMPOUNDS

DRUGS AND CHEMICAL TOXINS

Once the DNA of the insect has been analyzed, a chemical analysis can be conducted to reveal activities such as prior drug use or poisoning of the victim, plus factors that might influence the life cycles of the maggot, causing it to accelerate or hinder growth. Often as a consequence of decomposition—once blood urine and solid organs are no longer procurable—toxicological analysis is the only avenue of approach to ascertaining if the body came in contact with drugs or chemical toxins.

Insects can present IC analysts with useful information where a victim had been interrogated with the use of drugs, such as sodium pentothal (truth serum) or LSD; nevertheless, this claim has not clearly been validated in open sources. A toxicologist has to seek such drugs during toxicological analysis. Experts in the field of forensic entomology, such as Introna, have documented the presence of morphine in insect cases of opiate intoxication.[60] In addition, Gunatilake and Goff were able to confirm malathion poisoning by analysis of blowfly larvae from a decomposing body. [61] The following chemicals have been traced in maggots and the results are as noted:

---

[59] Starkeby, "Ultimate Guide to Forensic Entomology: Introduction to Forensic Entomology," 2004.

[60] F. Introna and others, "Opiate Analysis in Cadaveric Blowfly Larvae as an Indicator of Narcotic Intoxication," *Journal of Forensic Sciences* 35 (1990): 1.

[61] K. Gunatilake and M. L. Goff, "Detection of Organophosphate Poisoning in a Putrefying Body by Analyzing Arthropod Larvae," *Journal of Forensic Sciences* 34 (1989): 3.

Cocaine—high doses can accelerate the development of some sarcophagids.

Malathion—(insecticide) commonly used in suicide, usually taken orally by mouth, can delay the colonization of insects in the mouth.

Amitriptyline—(antidepressant) can prolong the development time up to 77 hours in one species of Sarcophagidae.[62]

One case that can shed some light on drugs and toxin analysis is that of a corpse found by bystanders walking in a wooded area in February 2004. Haskell and Catts explain that the decedent was a 29-year-old intravenous cocaine drug user who had been reported missing the prior day. "The body was found prone and skeletonized at the skull and trunk. The report revealed that no drugs or paraphernalia were found, to include no distinctive marks, cuts, tears, holes, or evidence of injury to reveal foul play. What was found on the decomposed body was small to large maggots (1st, 2nd, 3rd instars). Skeletal muscle along with maggots were submitted for toxicological analysis. Both tissue and maggots were identified as being positive for cocaine. Based on the facts related to the body, the cause of death was ruled overdose."[63]

In addition to telling the "true story," insects can provide valuable information regarding drug trafficking. Because illegal drugs are often made in one country and sold in others, it can be important to find out where the drugs were produced. Morten Starkeby explains that, sometimes, insects and other arthropods can be found together with the drugs.[64] A better explanation of this concept is set forth through a scenario: A brick of marijuana being shipped from Colombia, cultivated in a high-altitude location in the region, finds its way to America. While entering the U.S. the drugs are seized by Border Patrol agents. Further analysis reveals that a unique spider, found only in the high altitudes of the Colombian mountains, was found packed in the one-pound brick. This in turn leads investigators to the point of origin.

Starkeby adds, "If these insects are [identified], and the world distribution of the different insects is plotted on a map, one can, by analyzing the degree of overlap, find out approximately where the drugs came from. If one looks at the biology of the insect species found with the drugs, one can also often say something about the surroundings where the drugs were produced or packed."[65]

---

[62] Starkeby, "Ultimate Guide to Forensic Entomology: Introduction to Forensic Entomology," 2004.

[63] Haskell and Catts, 35-36.

[64] Starkeby, "Ultimate Guide to Forensic Entomology: Introduction to Forensic Entomology," 2004.

[65] Starkeby, "Ultimate Guide to Forensic Entomology: Introduction to Forensic Entomology," 2004.

BIOLOGICAL AGENTS AND
EXPLOSIVE COMPOUNDS

To date, the idea that forensic entomology could reveal valuable information pertaining to explosive residues found at or near death sites, which have or have not been reached in a timely manner, remains hypothetical. Cases relating to both DNA and drug transfer, through maggots, suggest a high probability (on a scale of low, medium, and high) of explosive compound and biological and chemical agent transfer.

A scenario that helps show the relevance of the explosive residue/maggot transfer theory—and might give insight to what analysts would be up against if policymakers had questions—is the case of an airline accident.

The question could be that, if technology should fail in the field, by what other means would investigators be able to find out if high explosives had been used? The answer in this case is forensic entomology and chemical analysis. The theory in this case is that forensic entomology, through chemical analysis, would be able to reveal if explosive residues were present on the body of a victim by analyzing the blowfly larvae and pupae.

Cases include that of U.S. Secretary of Commerce Ron Brown, Representative Mickey Leland of Texas, and Representative Larry McDonald of Georgia, all dying in plane crashes:

- **2 April 1996; U.S. Air Force 737-T43; near Dubrovnik, Croatia:** The aircraft struck mountainous terrain while attempting to land at the airport under conditions of reduced visibility. The flight crew was using an unapproved approach. All six crew members and 29 passengers were killed. Among the passengers were a number of U.S. corporate executives and the U.S. Secretary of Commerce, Ron Brown. The aircraft is a military version of the 737 that was used to transport military and civilian VIPs.

- **7 August 1989; Ethiopia:** Representative Mickey Leland of Texas was killed in a crash in Ethiopia.

- **1 September 1983; Korean Air Lines 747-200; near Sakhalin Island, Soviet Union:** Representative Larry McDonald of Georgia was killed along with 29 crew members and the other 239 passengers. The aircraft was shot down by at least one Soviet air-to-air missile after the 747 had strayed into Soviet airspace. [66]

Forensic entomology could in this case reveal valuable information about whether explosive compounds were found near or at death sites where badly decomposed bodies have not been reached in a timely manner. By obtaining body tissue—to include that of

---

[66] "Fatal Aircraft Events Involving U.S. Politicians," *AirSafe.com*, 26 October 2002, *MSN*, under the keyword "aircraft accidents involving U.S. politicians," URL: <http://www.cowjones.net/events/celebs/politics.html>," accessed 28 April 2004.

larvae found—and sending it to a chemical analysis lab, one should be able to assess whether a body has been exposed to an explosive compound. It is at this point that one can determine if foul play was in fact the cause of the crash. Upon identifying explosive materials during chemical analysis, comparative analysis can be conducted with known and unknown samples.

For example, larva samples from a previous bombing victim are submitted for chemical analysis and test positive for TNT. This sample can then be compared to an unknown sample of explosives recovered at another location (terrorist safehouse). If both samples reveal an identical chemical signature, one can ascertain a connection, thus proving the same explosive compounds were used by the same terrorist cell. This type of analysis is only possible if the insects are properly collected and taken to a professional forensic entomologist for extraction and chemical analysis.

To test the theory of explosive transfer through biological means and introduce new analytical tools to help solve terrorist bombings within the IC, the author conducted an experiment using TNT on porcine muscle in an uncontrolled outdoor and controlled indoor environment. The next section will discuss how the original E2 Project was conducted. One should note that this test had never been conducted before and will not only add to the science and research of forensic entomology but could also become a new analytical technique and tool for the IC to combat terrorist bombings and war crimes.

INITIATING THE ENTOMOLOGY/EXPLOSIVE (E2) PROJECT

To initiate the E2 Project, a plan was formulated. The plan would consist of two parts: (1) an outdoor uncontrolled environmental chamber (until maggots reached the 2nd instar), and (2) an indoor controlled environmental forensic laboratory chamber. Upon reaching the 3rd and pupa stage, maggots would then be macerated and sent to a toxicology lab for explosive analysis.

An outdoor fly-rearing chamber, or "maggot farm," was constructed using a 12" x 6" x 6" plastic container purchased at a local pet store. The initial rearing chamber contained one inch of kitty litter (bottom) and one inch of potting soil (top), placed in an outdoor uncontrolled environment. Two pieces of porcine muscle were placed in the chamber, side by side and one inch apart (one doped with TNT and the other without; see Figure 7). Explosives used in this experiment were purchased and obtained from Cerilliant. The compound used consisted of one pound of Trinitrotoluene (TNT) explosives.[67] The porcine muscle in this case was used to attract the unknown fly species found in the Alexandria, Virginia, area (see Figure 8). Once the larvae reached the 2nd instar stage, they would be prepared for transfer. This would conclude the first part of the two-part project. The second part would include transferring and rearing the maggots in a controlled forensic laboratory environment.

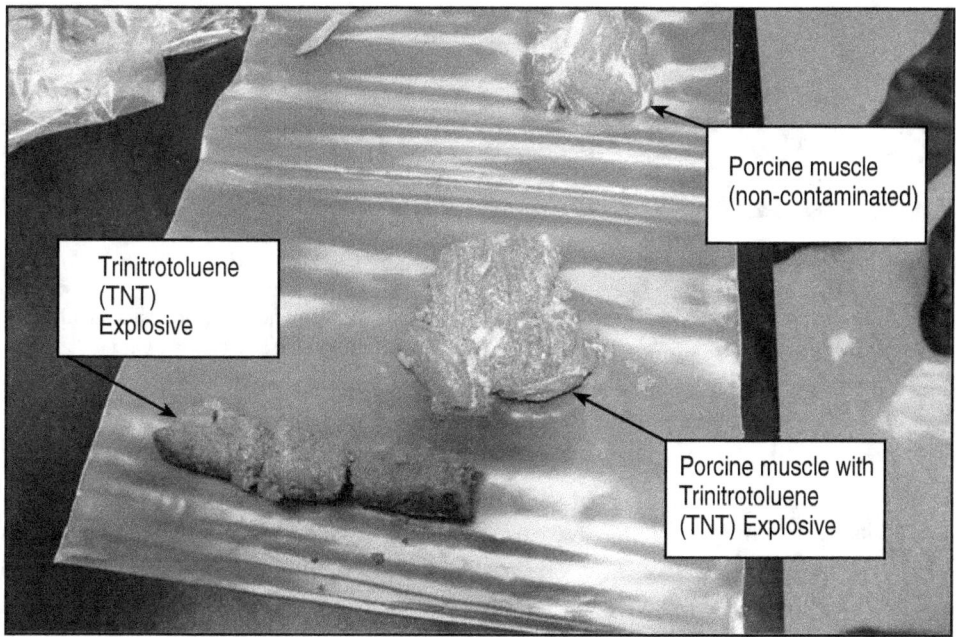

Figure 7. Porcine Muscle and One Pound Trinitrotoluene (TNT) Explosive (Bottom)

Explosive material (TNT) is highly toxic and produces a brown oily residue. Two samples of porcine muscle are noted, one with TNT (middle) and the other without (top). Photographed 21 April 2004.

Source: Author's Analysis.

---

[67] Cerilliant Explosive Company, phone number 1-800-848-7837. Trinitrotoluene (TNT) explosives were utilized in explosive entomology project, CAS No 118-96-7, $20.00 plus shipping.

Porcine muscle

One inch vermiculite

One inch potting soil

Porcine muscle meat containing TNT

Figure 8. Day One. Fly Rearing Chamber

Note the location of the one inch kitty litter (bottom) and one inch potting soil (top). This simulates a natural setting for larvae burrowing. Porcine muscle is set on top of the soil and is being utilized for live specimens experiment, photographed 0700 hours 7 May 2004.

Source: Author's Analysis.

Upon completing the first part of the project, blowfly egg oviposit on the porcine muscle and larvae reaching the 2nd instar would be transported via automobile to the forensic laboratory of the Office of the Armed Forces Medical Examiner (AFME) in Rockville, Maryland. There instars (larvae) would then be transferred and placed in two transparent plastic containers (18" in circumference x 6" tall), each containing a piece of fresh porcine muscle (one doped with TNT and the other without). In addition, one pound of ready-to-use vermiculite soil was placed in the rearing chamber to simulate a natural setting and allow 3rd instars to burrow (see Figure 16). The experiment was then photographed and plastic containers placed in a temperature-regulated forensic evidence cabinet to be reared (see Figure 20).

Rearing information was obtained from the first forensic entomology textbook, published in 1986 by Smith, and the second in 1990 by Haskell and Catts. Both texts were a primary source of information throughout the planning process and the project. Shorter articles are also available on forensic entomology, often authored by the same two expert contributors.

A Washington, DC, expert in the field of forensic entomology and forensic anthropology was consulted on multiple occasions via telephone for his technical expertise and guidance. The expert contacted was Dr. William C. Rodriguez, Chief, Deputy Medical Examiner of the Armed Forces Medical Examiner Special Investigations Office[68] Questions asked were unofficial and considered informal. The majority of questions asked during the project concerned the rearing and transferability of maggots during the entomology/explosive project. Dr. Rodriguez presented the fundamental foundation and gave sound advice to initiate and carry out the original entomology/explosive detection project.

EQUIPMENT USED DURING THE EXPERIMENT

The following equipment was purchased and used in the experiment to establish the time of the fly's larviposit and stages of development (instars):

---

[68] William C. Rodriguez III, Ph.D., Chief, Deputy Medical Examiner, Office of the Armed Forces Medical Examiner (AFME), Rockville, MD. Telephone interview by the author, 8 June 2004.

1. One pair of surgical rubber gloves.

2. Forceps to handle specimens on the porcine muscle.

3. One surgical knife.

4. One small artist paint brush for picking up tiny specimens that might be damaged by forceps.

5. One 10"/25 cm net, fishing type, for collecting flying insects in the air or on a corpse.

6. Plastic container, 12" x 6" x 6," with ventilated lid.

7. Plastic container, 18" in circumference x 6" height, with ventilated lid.

8. One pound of potting soil.

9. One pound of kitty litter.

10. One pound of ready-to-use vermiculite top soil.

11. Specimen, consisting of one pound of porcine muscle (with collection jars for specimens, containing 70 percent Isopropyl alcohol as a killing agent).

12. Isopropyl alcohol (70 percent).

13. One six-inch ruler with straight edge.

14. Camera, specifically a Canon 35 mm.

15. Kodak Max 800 Versatile Plus color film.

16. One pound of Trinitrotoluene (TNT) explosives.

17. Five transparent plastic trays, 4" x 4."

18. Black screen, 4' x 4.'

19. One box of large rubber bands.

20. Calliphoraidae, or green bottle blowflies (unknown number).

Keep in mind that in the first part of the experiment a colony of larvae was reared to the 2nd instar stage (adult flies were utilized to lay eggs on the porcine muscle in an uncontrolled temperature and environment), located in the Alexandria, Virginia, area. Upon reaching the 2nd instar, on day five, the second part of the experiment began. Larvae were transported and reared for nine more days in a controlled environmental chamber located at the Office of the Armed Forces Medical Examiner, Forensic Laboratories, in Rockville, Maryland, on 11 May 2004 (see Figures 9-20).

Before chemical analysis could be accomplished, the porcine muscle in both circumstances—from the uncontrolled outdoor environment and the controlled environmental chamber—was doped with TNT explosive. This simulates carrion feeding on a body that has been exposed to an explosive compound during a bombing (e.g., where the body came in contact with residue from a detonated IED).

The first part of the experiment was uncontrolled. The experiment was placed outdoors near a high-rise building in Alexandria. Sunlight illuminated the larvae from the east, giving the chamber 12 hours of sunlight exposure. Shrubs near the building provided visual cover and natural shade during daylight hours. The chamber contained one inch of potting soil on top and one inch of kitty litter on the bottom. The substance would help to absorb liquids and odor. This would also simulate a natural setting and allow the instar larvae to burrow. On 7 May 2004 at 0700 hours the experiment started. Daily recordings were conducted on behavior patterns, time, day, temperature, and humidity readings. Upon the larvae reaching 2nd instar (Day Five of the project), they were transferred to a temperature- and humidity-controlled environment chamber.

The second part of the experiment would start at 1400 hours on Day Five, 11 May 2004. The oviposit of fly eggs and larvae from the uncontrolled experiment were placed in a small circular experimental chamber to establish contact with the fresh porcine muscle. The second rearing site provided 24 hours of controlled temperature in a room at 85 degrees Fahrenheit and 60 percent relative humidity. Other factors of control included 12 hours of light and 12 hours of darkness—simulating natural light—continuous airflow, moisture, and protection from predaceous insects and animals.

At the 3rd instar stage, larvae were extracted with forceps and bathed first in hot water (170 degrees), then in a 90 percent ethanol solution to rid the larvae of any external contaminants that could give false residual TNT readings when analyzed. After bathing, larvae were crushed using a glass pestle. The macerated remains were then dried under an infrared heat lamp for eight hours, which resulted in a dry residue. Residue was then scraped and placed into a glass vial and sent to the Department of Environmental Toxicology and Pathology for analysis. There a Scanning Electron Microscope with an Energy Dispersive X-Ray Spectroscopy machine (SEM/EDAX) was utilized to identify properties and elements within the macerated maggots' tissues.

Scanning Electron Microscope with Energy Dispersive X-Ray Spectroscopy

The scanning electron microscope has automated features, to include auto focus/auto stigmator, and automatic contrast and brightness. The system is expandable, addressing needs from morphological observation to multipurpose, high-resolution elemental analysis.

The unique signature, if found, could help investigators and analysts pinpoint unique explosive materials at different locales. For example, explosive material found at a terrorist safehouse may be related to a known bombing. Chemical entomology/explosive analysis may be the link to connect the two if the signatures match, just as fingerprints are used at a crime scene. The SEM/EDAX system is required to determine whether elements of TNT can be found and if explosive transferability via entomological means is possible.

Fresh porcine muscle, non-contminated (left) and meat covered with TNT (right)

Figure 9. Day One. Initial Exposure

Exposure of uncontrolled outdoor experiment conducted in Alexandria, VA. Porcine muscle subjected to TNT is located on the right. Porcine muscle has been exposed outdoors for less than five minutes. Note the initial brown discoloration of TNT. Strong toxic odor is present. Photographed 0705 hours, 7 May 2004.

Source: Author's Analysis.

Blowfly present within
one hour, five minutes

Figure 10. Day One. Green Bottle Blowfly Present

Blowfly is present within one hour, time 0805. Blowfly is tolerant of the TNT porcine sample and is not affected by strong toxic odor it presents. Photographed 7 May 2004.

Source: Author's Analysis.

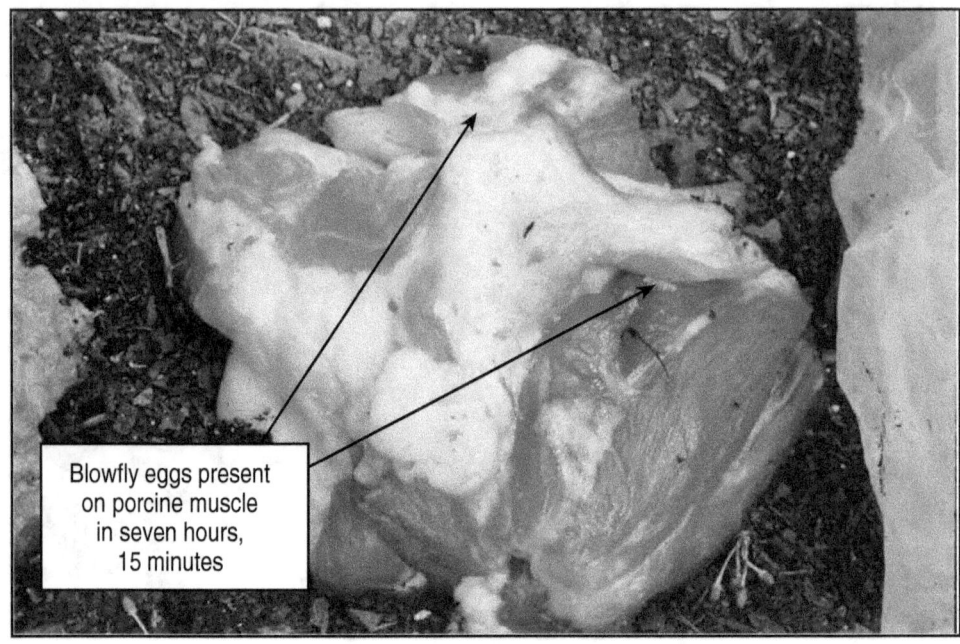

Blowfly eggs present
on porcine muscle
in seven hours,
15 minutes

Figure 11. Day One. Fly Eggs Present

Blowfly eggs are white in appearance, present on non-contaminated porcine muscle (middle right corner, under lip of fat). Eggs present on porcine muscle confirm blowfly's ability to lay eggs near TNT compound. Photographed 1415 hours, 7 May 2004.

Source: Author's Analysis.

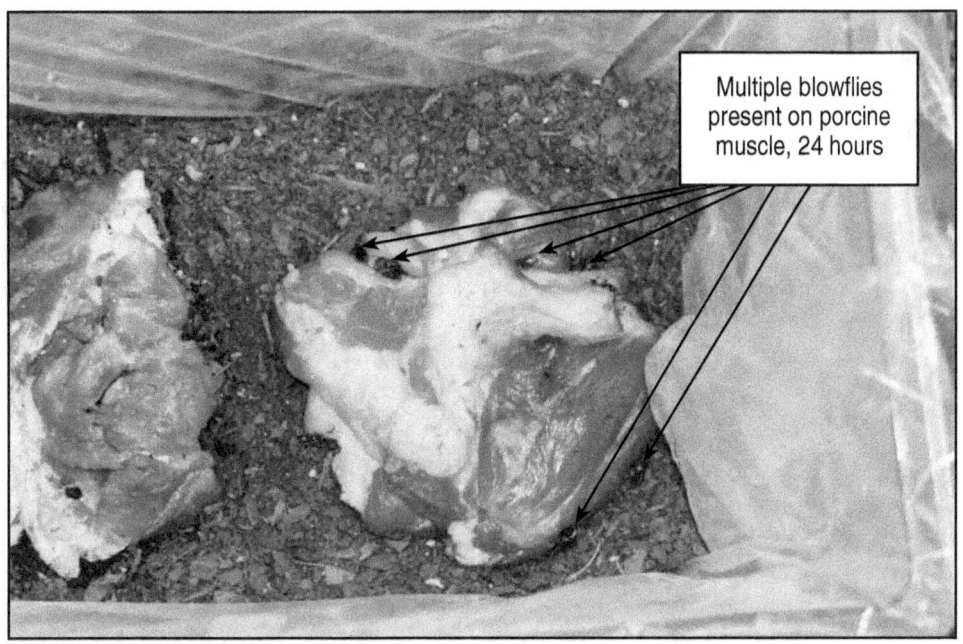

Multiple blowflies present on porcine muscle, 24 hours

Figure 12. Day Two. Multiple Green Bottle Blowflies Present

Presence of flies confirms the fly's ability to smell rotting meat exposed in an outdoor environment. Photographed 0700 hours, 8 May 2004.

Source: Author's Analysis.

1st instar larvae mass
within 25 hours,
30 minutes

Figure 13. Day Two. Mass Green Bottle Blowfly Larvae Present (1st Instar Stage)

Note mass formation of larvae under the left corner of the uncontaminated porcine muscle. Eggs are
white in appearance. Photographed 0830 hours, 8 May 2004.

Source: Author's Analysis.

Figure 14. Day Three. Decomposing Porcine Muscle

Green bottle blowflies present. Major discoloration on porcine muscle with TNT, brown to dark brown. No maggots present, burrowed under meat due to container being exposed to sunlight. Note rapid decomposition of porcine muscle with TNT. Photographed 0700 hours, 9 May 2004.

Source: Author's Analysis.

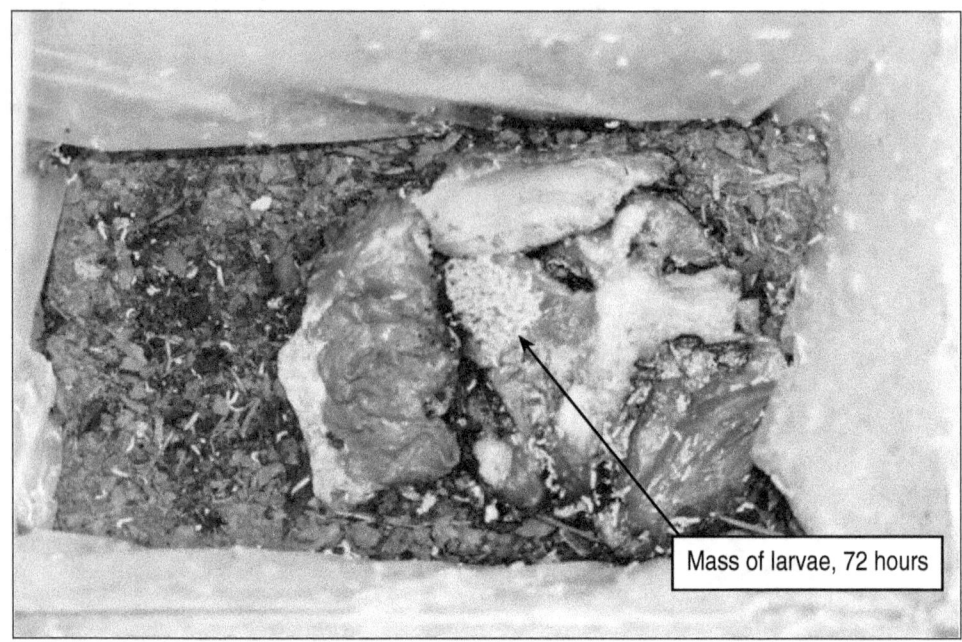

Figure 15. Day Four. Porcine Muscle in Active Decay

2nd stage larvae and green bottle blowflies are present. Note leather discoloration on porcine muscle with TNT. Larvae are highly active and behavior is erratic. Larvae have introduced themselves to the contaminated TNT porcine muscle. Note larvae massed in center and around plastic in container. Photographed 0700 hours, 10 May 2004.

Source: Author's Analysis.

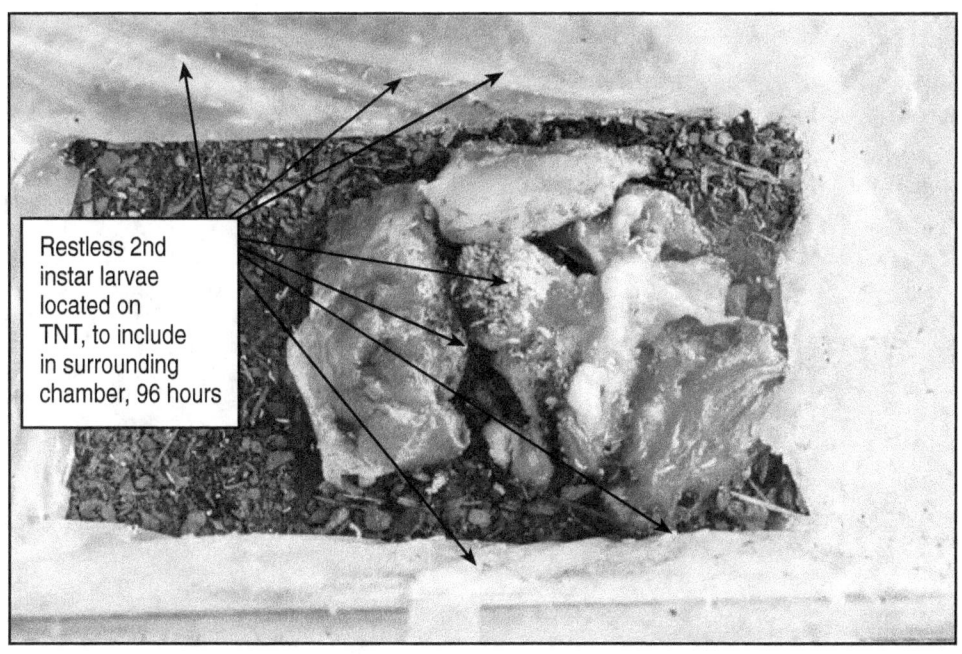

Restless 2nd
instar larvae
located on
TNT, to include
in surrounding
chamber, 96 hours

Figure 16. Day Five. 2nd Instars Present

Instars surround the chamber in an uncontrolled environment. Larvae samples shown are taken from chamber and reared in a controlled environment at the Office of the Armed Forces Medical Examiner. Photographed 0700 hours, 11 May 2004.

Source: Author's Analysis.

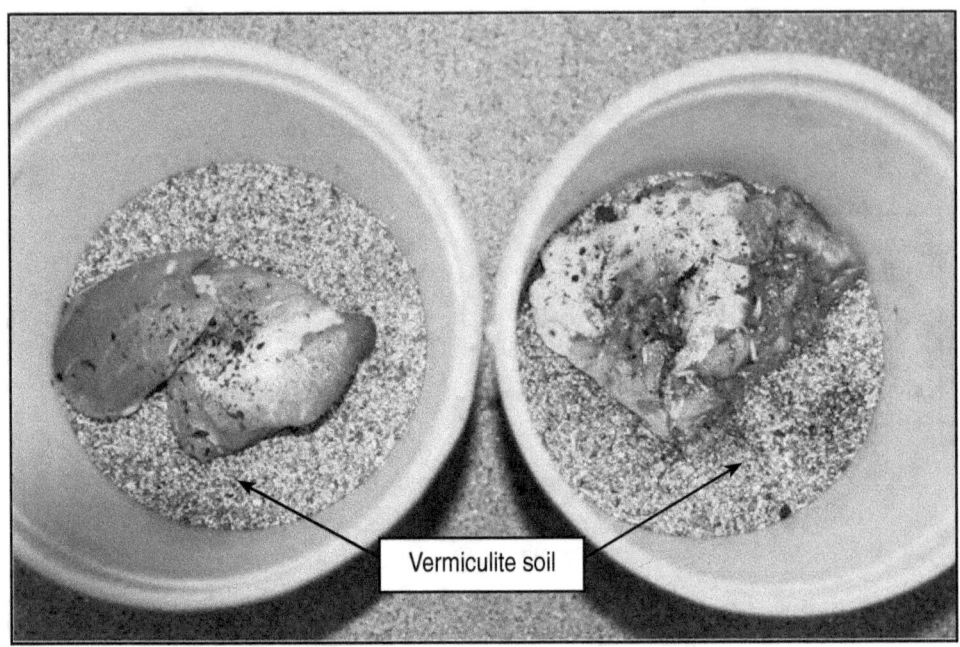

Figure 17. Day Five. Transfer of Larvae to the Forensic Lab

11 May 2004, 2nd and 3rd instars were introduced to new porcine muscle. Porcine muscle without TNT is located on the left and porcine muscle with TNT is on the right. Larvae samples are in a controlled environment and are being reared at the Office of the Armed Forces Medical Examiner. Photographed 1500 hours, 11 May 2004.

Source: Author's Analysis.

Figure 18. Day Five. 2nd and 3rd Instar Transfer

Rearing transfer containers contain porcine muscle (one container with TNT). Transfer of larvae was successful. Container contains ventilated top (mesh wire). Photographed 1500 hours, 11 May 2004.

Source: Author's Analysis.

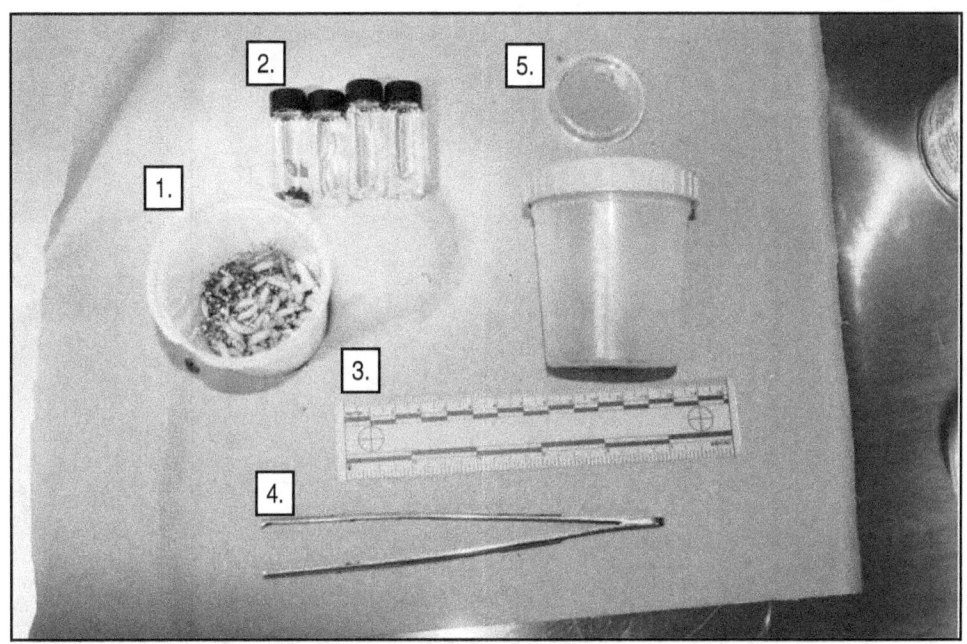

Figure 19. Day Twelve. Containers and
Tools used for transfer and collection are shown above.

(1) Plastic bottles with resealable lids (located on left/center) contain live 2nd and 3rd instar larvae. Bottle is utilized for collection and easy access to instars. (2) Smaller specimen jars (top left) with black resealable lids are also utilized for sampling and preserving. Jars are made of glass and contain half Isopropyl alcohol (70 percent) and half hot water, 170 degrees in Fahrenheit. (3) Six-inch ruler (bottom) was used to measure specimens. (4) Forceps (bottom) were utilized to delicately handle specific specimens (instars) located in the plastic containers when needed. (5) Lastly, circular transparent plastic resealable container (top right) was used to view and identify larvae specimens under a microscope. Note, the larvae contained in the plastic container (mid-left) were rinsed with hot water, then bathed in 90 percent ethanol solution, macerated, and sent to the Armed Forces Medical Examiner and the Department of Environmental and Toxicological Pathology. Chemical analysis would reveal if in fact the TNT explosive compound could be extracted from the larvae fat content. Photo of tools and containers taken at the Office of the Armed Forces Medical Examiner, forensic laboratory. 1530 hours, 18 May 2004.

Source: Author's Analysis.

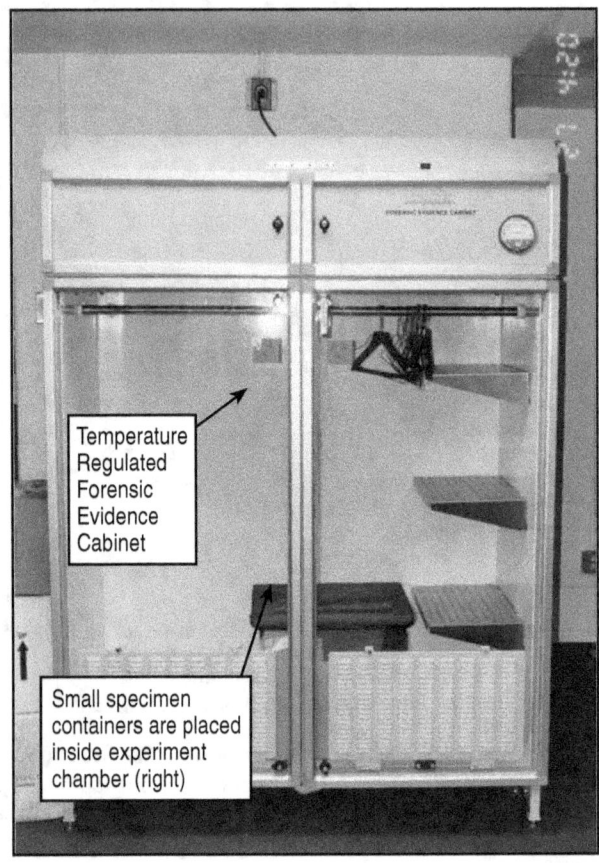

Figure 20. Temperature-Regulated Forensic Evidence Cabinet

Live larvae specimen container is placed in experiment rearing chamber. Chamber is then placed in Forensic Evidence Cabinet where the temperature is controlled to 85 degrees Fahrenheit with 60 percent relative humidity. Photographed 27 March 2004.

Source: Author's Analysis.

IDENTIFICATION OF THE FAUNA

On 18 May 2004, the larvae reared were visually and properly identified under a microscope as Calliphoraidae species, green bottle blowfly.[69] The larva's posterior spiracles, containing three lines, were viewed to determine species. Such features of insects can be found in Haskell and Catts, *Procedural Guide to Forensic Entomology*. The features of the green bottle blowfly are distinctive:

---

[69] Smith, 92.

1. Thorax has three cross grooves and black bristle-like hair, usually with a brilliant blue-green metallic tail end.

2. Abdomen generally green-striped, banded, or spotted pattern.

3. Reddish eyes.

4. Strongly bristled hair on legs, thorax, and abdomen.

Figure 21. Calliphoraidae, Green Bottle Blowfly

Source: James L. Castner, "Ultimate Guide to Forensic Entomology: A Review of Forensic Identification Cards," Web-only essay, URL: <http://folk.uio.no/mostarke/forens_ent/ reviewFIFC.html>, accessed 20 March 2004. Used with permission.

The green bottle blowflies are diverse in their feeding habits, but are united in the association of their maggots with animal tissue (living or dead) or animal dung. Behavioral characteristics of the green bottle blowfly and its larvae are as follows:

1. Deposits eggs instead of live larvae on cadavers.

2. Scavenger, predator or parasitoid of insects, spiders and their egg sacs, snails, and earthworms.

3. Dung feeders.

4. Carrion feeders, including vertebrate and invertebrate (human or animal) carrion.[70]

After identifying species, ambient temperature recordings and samples of insects were collected twice a day, at 0700 hours and 1700 hours, until flies pupated (see Appendix). Once pupated and adult fly emergence occurred, recordings were reduced to once a day starting at 0700 hours. Photographs were taken during recording periods to establish decay cycles of the host and to measure maggots, pupae, and adults.

The data compiled from this experiment provide a brief description of the life cycle of the green bottle blowfly in a Mediterranean environment. This study reveals rate of meta-

---

[70] J. Ohara, "Arthropods Associated With Livestock Dung," Web-only essay, URL: <http:// res.agr.ca/ ecorc/apss/arthback.htm>, accessed 8 October 2003.

morphosis, reactions and behavior characteristics to TNT, and reactions to sunlight and variant temperatures. More importantly, data reveal if explosive residues can be extracted from larva fat reserves. The results of the toxicology report conducted by the Armed Forces Medical Examiner's Office may help intelligence officials develop alternative methods of gathering explosive data at a crime scene, when other means cease to prevail.

RESULTS OF THE ENTOMOLOGY/EXPLOSIVE (E2) PROJECT

Depending on weather conditions, a dead body that lies above ground will normally be quickly consumed by insects and their larvae. The body of an adult human may be completely consumed in as little as six months after death. A child's body may take only a month.[71] A piece of pork, which was the basis of this research, took two weeks to be consumed.

The experimental rearing of green bottle blowflies and analysis of porcine muscle for 17 days (one doped with TNT and the other sample without), revealed that green bottle blowflies do have a successive life cycle and *will* consume meat exposed to explosive compounds. The E2 Project experiment and toxicological laboratory analysis provides empirical evidence that explosive compounds could be transferred biologically and identified by obtaining blowfly larva samples.

Blowfly larvae have demonstrated the ability to store numerous substances in their bodies which transfer during feeding of mammalian tissues. The same concept applies to explosive compounds. As the body decomposes, many of these compounds, whether drugs or explosives, break down into the tissues. At times the body's main organs could be badly decomposed and toxic substances on the surface could have been degraded or eaten by predators (i.e., animals), thus making the corpse itself unsuitable for toxicological analysis. Thus, the witness that can help find the answer or "ground truth" for analysts charged with resolving any case involving war crimes or terrorist activities is the blowfly larvae. The blowfly can help in the detection of drugs, chemical toxins, and explosive compounds. This is possible due to the larvae eating the dermal tissue and internal organs (see Figure 22).

---

[71] V. Geberth, *Practical Homicide Investigation: Tactics, Procedures, and Forensic Techniques* (New York: Boca Raton, 1993), 44.

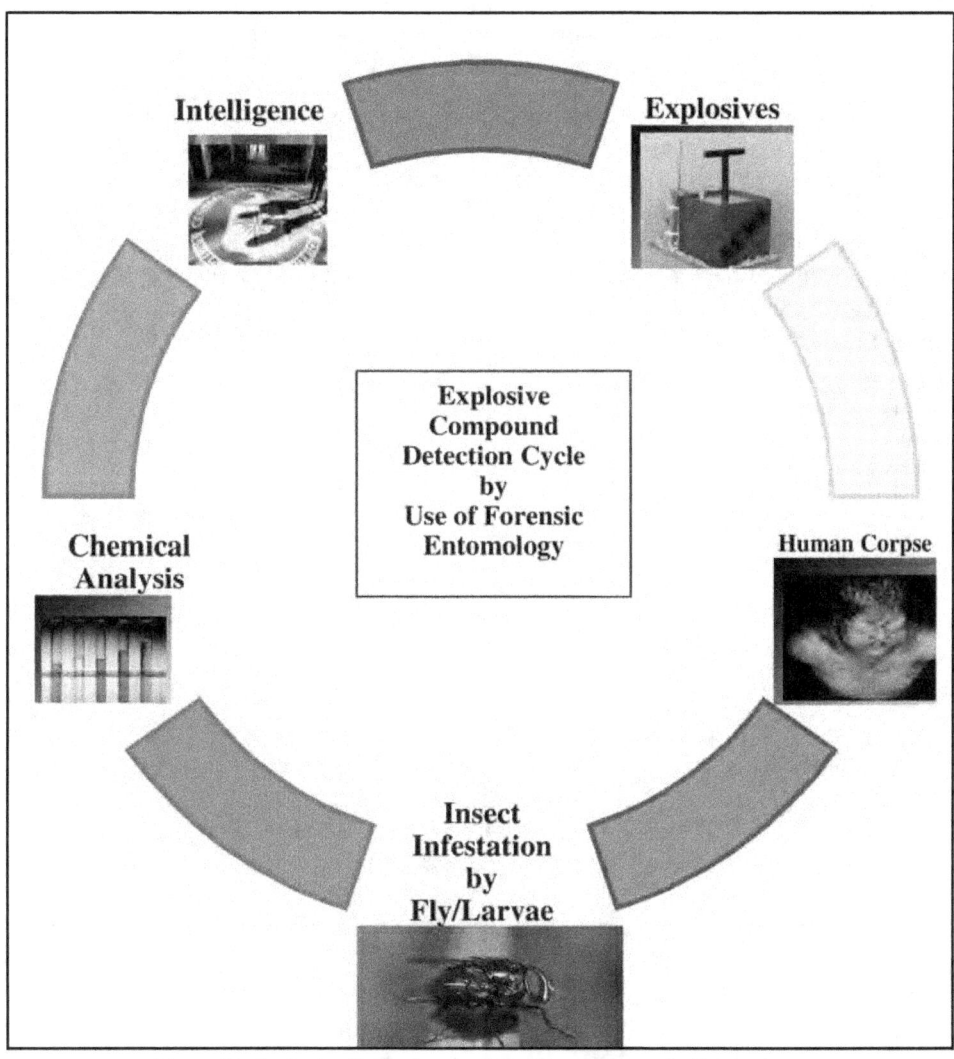

Figure 22. Explosive Detection Cycle by Use of Forensic Entomology

Source: Author's Analysis.

In this E2 Project, TNT explosive was the compound that was introduced to the blow-fly larva and was later identified through chemical analysis, showing that explosive transfer and extraction *can* be accomplished through biological means.

CHEMICAL ANALYSIS

To certify explosive transferability through larvae, hard evidence is provided and explained by chemical analysis. Explosive material analysis was conducted 24 May 2004 at the Armed Forces Medical Examiner's Office to reveal if an explosive compound, specifically

Trinitrotoluene (TNT) explosive, was present in the 2nd and 3rd instar stage (larva). Larvae extracted from the experiment were cleansed first in hot water (170 degrees), then bathed in 90 percent ethanol solution prior to toxicological examination.

The data revealed from the SEM/EDAX were based on a count of 0-1000 and energy reading of 0-10 for elements reflected on the Periodic Table. The examined macerated sample of larvae, which were reared on porcine muscle without TNT, contained elements which are normally found in maggots to sustain life (oxygen, calcium, potassium, etc.). On the other hand, the larva sample reared on porcine muscle containing TNT, when compared to the non-TNT sample, contained the same elements to sustain life, but also included a very high count of metal elements (iron, aluminum, magnesium, etc.) and silicon (see Figures 23 and 24).

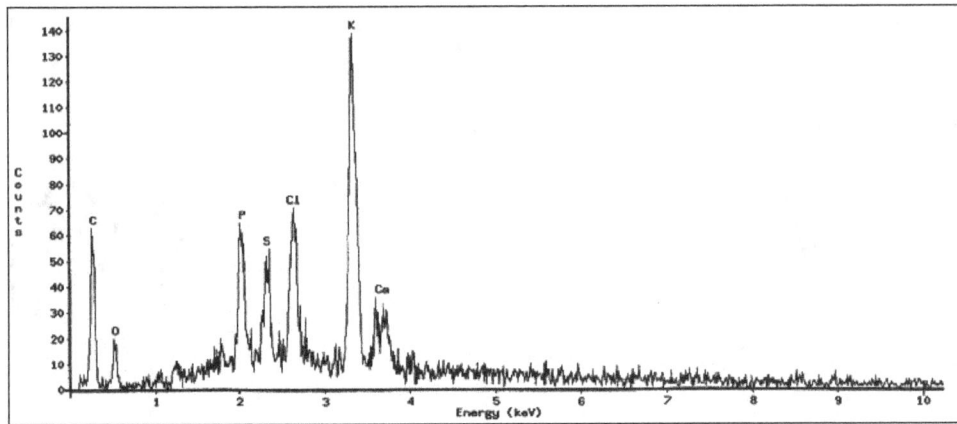

Figure 23. Chemical Analysis of Non-TNT Larva Sample

Source: Author's Analysis.

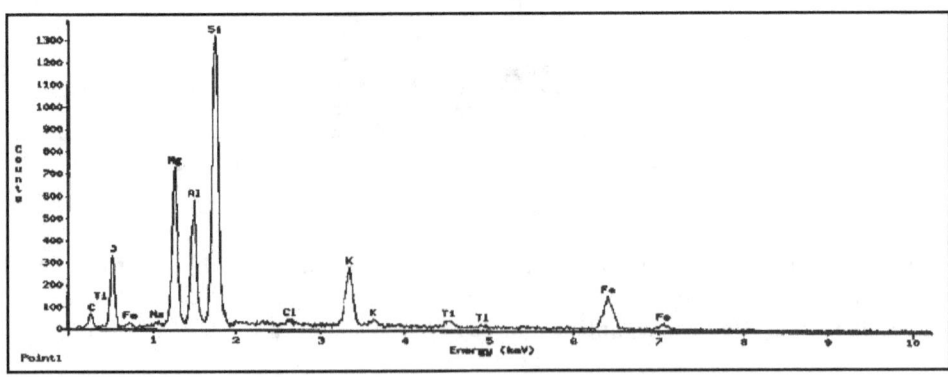

Figure 24. Chemical Analysis of TNT Larva Sample

Note high metallic elements (by-products of TNT). See key to elements shown on chart above in Table 3 below.

Source: Author's Analysis.

Non-TNT Sample.	TNT Sample.
C= Carbon	C= Carbon
O= Oxygen	O= Oxygen
P= Phosphorus	P= Phosphorus
S= Sulfur	S= Sulfur
Cl= Chlorine	Cl= Chlorine
K= Potassium	K= Potassium
Ca= Calcium	
	Mg= Magnesium
	Al=Aluminum
	Si= Silicon
	Ti= Titanium
	Fe= Iron
	Na= Sodium

Table 2. Key Elements Found in E2 Project Samples

Source: Author's Analysis.

These metals constitute evidence of by-products or by-components left within the larva's system, which can be used to identify explosives if no other means are available or if a secondary method is needed to confirm explosive identification. In this experimental case, the signature for TNT is noted and can be used to identify that specific batch, just as with a fingerprint. In an explosive identification case, this fingerprint (chemical signature) can then be used and compared to an unknown source of TNT. If both are identical in nature and elements are peaking at the same count, it can be concluded with high probability that both compounds came from the same manufacturer, location, and user.

BEHAVIORAL CHARACTERISTICS

Behavioral characteristics during the experiment were noted daily. Daylight exposure and eating habits during the 1st to 3rd instar stages were different. The maggots exhibited less tolerance to bright light with increasing age. Newly deposited larvae remained close to their deposition site regardless of the light for 8 to 10 hours, but soon afterward they tended to avoid the light, eating and gaining size for the rest of the larval period and into the prepupal stage, where burrowing and fasting were more common until pupation.

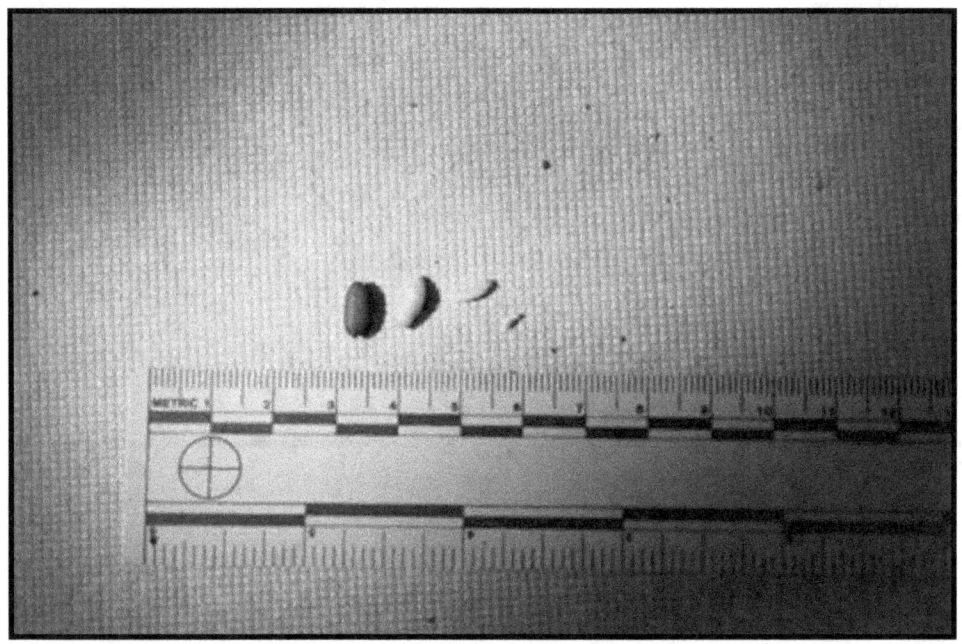

Figure 25. Day Twelve. 1st, 2nd, 3rd Instars, and Pupae

Photographed at the Armed Forces Medical Examiner's Office, 1400 hours, 18 May 2004.

Source: Author's Analysis.

Calliphoraidae (green bottle blowfly) 1st, 2nd, 3rd larval instars and pupae show significant growth and confirm the blowfly's life cycle to estimate PMI (see Figure 25). All were placed into tubes with the aid of forceps and preserved in a glass jar with 70 percent isopropyl alcohol and warm water for later study. Warm water was first utilized to stabilize proteins and kill larvae prior to transfer in half 70 percent isopropyl alcohol and half warm water.

On the fourth and fifth day of the experiment, during the second stage of porcine muscle decay, 2nd instar larvae were highly active and were found on the porcine muscle containing TNT as far as 12" from the main mass of larvae and inside of the experimental container. This reflects that the 2nd instar of the Calliphoraidae species no doubt has a keen ability to seek out new burrowing locations in a controlled outdoor environment (see Figure 26).

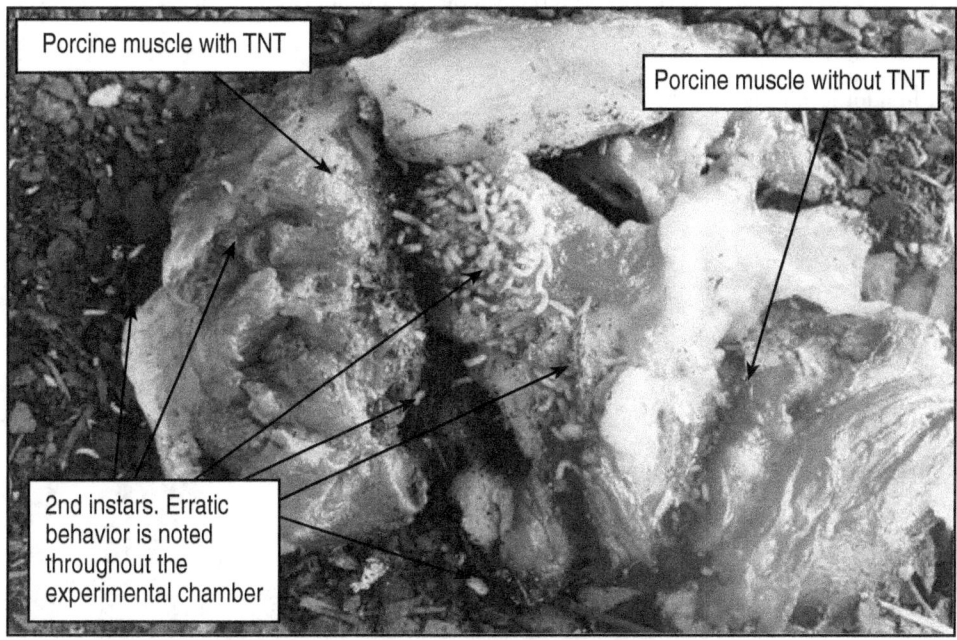

Porcine muscle with TNT

Porcine muscle without TNT

2nd instars. Erratic behavior is noted throughout the experimental chamber

Figure 26. Day Five. Instar Behavior on Porcine Muscle

Behavior is erratic and maggots are everywhere. Maggots are not affected by TNT. Photographed at the Armed Forces Medical Examiner's Office, 1400 hours, 11 May 2004.

Source: Author's Analysis.

After 20 days, three flies in the experimental container were set free. The fact that flies had been reared to adults in 17 days—normally 29 days at an average temperature of 70 degrees—may lead one to conclude the possibility that fly growth was enhanced by the TNT exposure in the uncontrolled outdoor chamber. Haskell and Catts' book *Entomology and Death* describes research which has associated a very accelerated development of maggots feeding on cocaine.[72] Nonetheless, more research in the area of explosive compounds and entomology will be needed to analyze this rapid growth theory.

The present research and analysis shows that the Calliphoraidae species (green bottle blowfly) that invaded both pieces of porcine muscle (one doped with TNT and one without) did so in a definite order of succession (see Table 3). To better understand the table, if an investigator were to find 2nd instars, 3rd instars, and pupae on the remains of a cadaver, it could be concluded from Table 4 that the instars occurred at different times. To simplify the PMI process one needs to look at the timeline of the various instar stages. Thus, the careful observation and collection of data on site, coupled with biological knowledge of

---

[72] Haskell and Catts, 36-37.

the insect concerned, will enable a reconstruction of events to be made including an estimated time of death (see Figure 27).

In addition, although the exact species of fauna may differ from country to country, from habitat to habitat, and from season to season, the basic pattern of succession of insects is remarkably constant around the world.

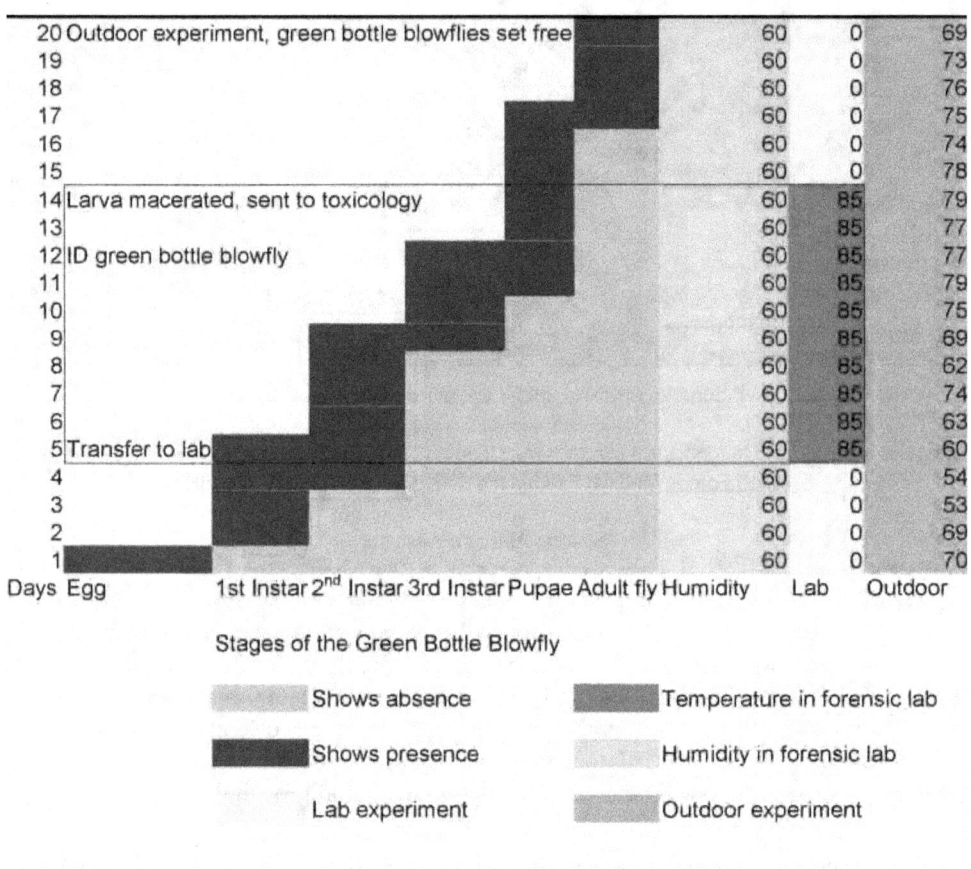

Table 3. Stages of the Calliphoraidae Species

The table shows results of the green bottle blowfly with one pound Trinitrotoluene (TNT) explosive.

Source: Author's Analysis.

56

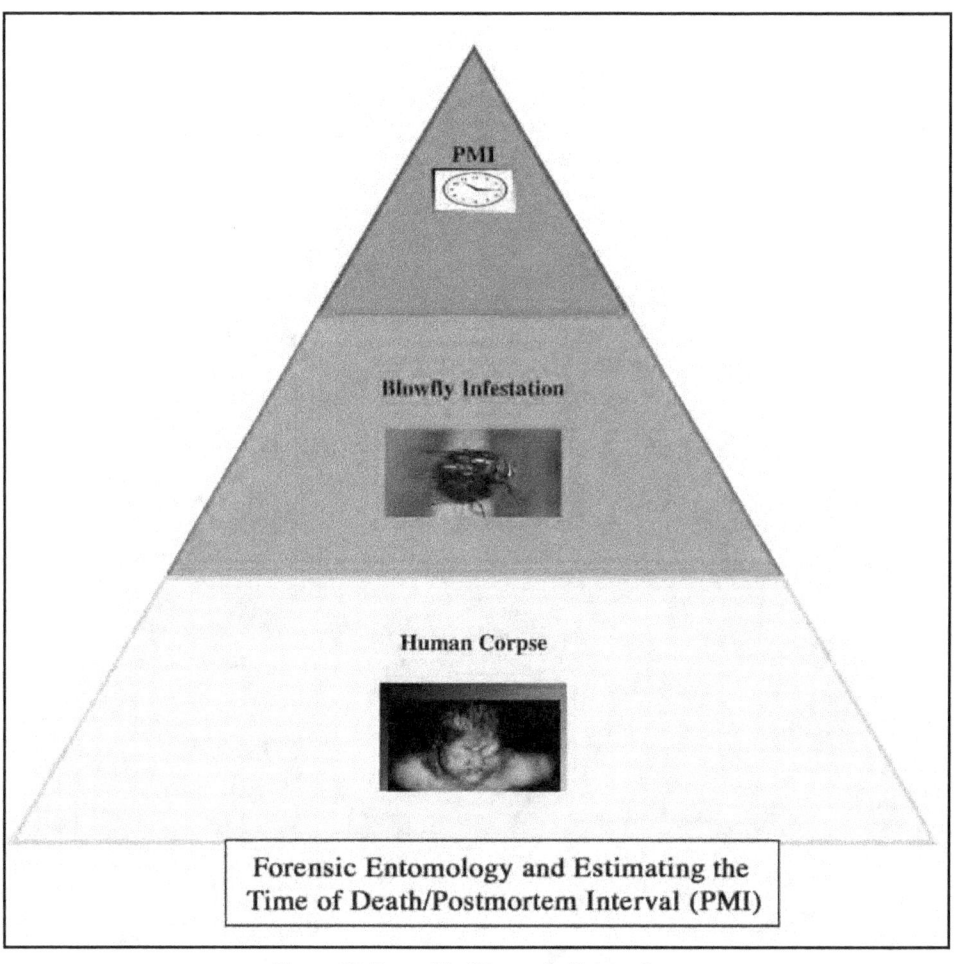

Figure 27. Pyramid of Forensic Entomology

Estimating the Time of Death/Postmortem Interval (PMI). Fly infestation on corpse allows one to estimate the time of death. This pyramid reflects the chain of evidentiary exploration, from broad, general evidence at the time of the discovery of a human corpse, to more specific evidence when blowfly infestation is detected, to determining the specific PMI after detailed analysis of all the evidence available.

Source: Author's Analysis.

THE E2 PROJECT AND THE
INTELLIGENCE COMMUNITY

This newly tested explosive detection technique can bring a new capability to the IC, both in a domestic and an international setting, by providing analysts and ultimately policymakers with unbiased answers as to what happened during explosive incidents. The forensic entomology application could reveal time of death, drug inducement, drug trafficking, and movement of the body in cases relating to war crimes or deliberate deception. In addition, the findings can be used as evidentiary leverage in cases where a leader has abused his power and has introduced forces in a country where they are committing atrocities against humanity. In light of the present experimental findings, PMI can also be assessed more thoroughly than before.

Figure 28 indicates the value of forensic entomology and its applicability to the IC.

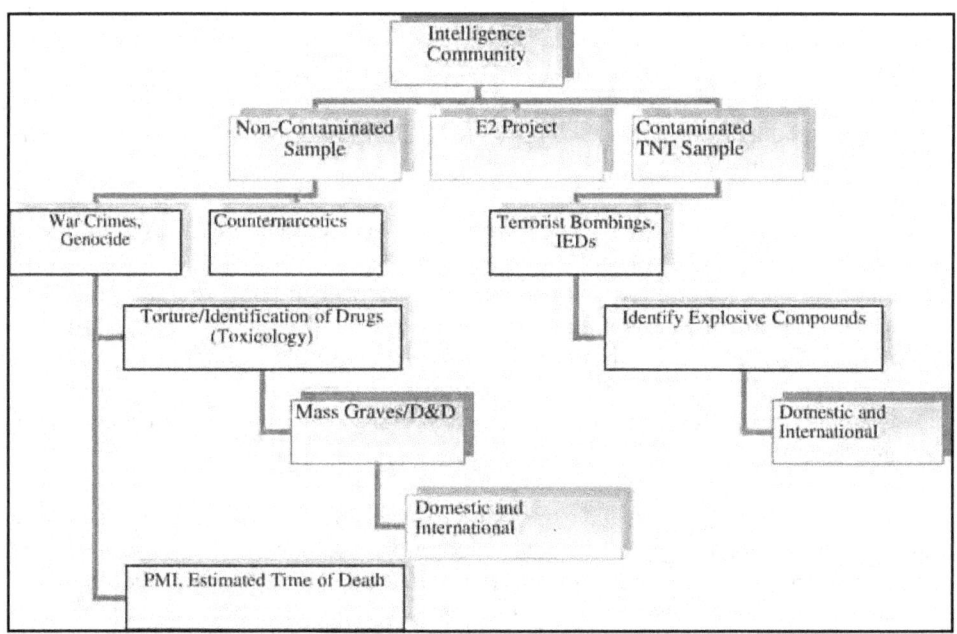

Figure 28. Applicability of the Forensic E2 Project to the IC

Source: Author's Analysis.

IMPLICATIONS

Real and perceived barriers in the past have kept law enforcement and intelligence agencies apart. Since 9/11 the barrier has been lifted; the U.S. Congress passed and the President signed a new law—the Uniting and Strengthening America by Providing Appropriate Tools Required to Intercept and Obstruct Terrorism Act of 2001 (USA PATRIOT Act).[73] Foreign intelligence information between the federal intelligence community and the federal law enforcement community could now be shared. With the onset of global terrorism, law enforcement and intelligence agencies can now join together, find new techniques, new technologies, new analytical methods, and implement them to fight the new borderless wars against global terrorism and war crimes. One law enforcement technique or tool is addressed in this study: forensic entomology.

The earlier historical discussion noted that, while insects have roamed the earth for 250 million years, forensic entomology has only come into being within the past few years. Insects interact with us in so many ways and in such different locales that we have often come to ignore them. Insects, primarily blowflies, are attracted to the smell of death and seek out the corpse to lay eggs and live off the body. Insects can provide us with a natural clock when someone's death triggers this activity. By studying the life cycle, we as investigators and analysts are able to estimate PMI and find the difficult answers to how and when the death occurred.

It is clear from this study that insects are a valuable asset to the IC. They are important because insects are like small intelligence agents; they are the first to discover a corpse, particularly if a person or a force has attempted to hide a body or bodies. As noted in the first part of the experiment, blowflies arrive and begin laying eggs on a body within minutes of death. They also arrive in succession, arriving at different times during decomposition. Although the exact species of fauna may differ from country to country and season to season, the basic succession of insects remains consistent around the world (flies, beetles, ants, etc.).

In case of genocide, mass clandestine graves are usually involved, but with the application of forensic entomology as a counter-deception tool one can unweave the web of denial and deception.[74] A murder victim transported to another location may show signs consistent only with the original location. Because different species have different habitat preferences and are also seasonal—for example, one species of green bottle fly, Lucilia sericata, prefers well-lit areas when breeding, while the black blowfly Phormia regina prefers shade[75]—awareness of such can help determine if in fact movement has occurred.

---

[73] Jeff Tandahl, "The USA Patriot Act," Electronic Privacy Information Center, URL: <http://www.epic.org/privacy/terrorism/usapatriot/>, accessed 8 June 2004.

[74] Scott Gerwehr and Russell W. Glen, *Unweaving the Web: Deception and Adaptation in Future Urban Operations* (Monterey, CA: Rand, 2002), Summary.

[75] May R. Barenbaum, *Ninety-Nine More Maggots, Mites, and Munchers* (Urbana and Chicago: University of Illinois Press, 1985), 10-46.

The E2 Project was conducted to answer the question if blowfly larvae could transfer explosive compounds via ingestion. On 24 May 2004 it was determined through chemical analysis that maggots could absorb explosive residues and compounds in their body. In addition, research revealed these compounds or metabolic byproducts can be detected in the laboratory. The rearing cycle of the green bottle blowflies proved to be invaluable. Research revealed that the larvae in fact ate the porcine muscle with TNT, and did so in a definite succession. We can infer that other high-explosive substances (RDX, HMX, SENTEX), as well as biological agents and other chemical substances, can be detected in the same manner. Collecting, rearing, and extracting fly larva tissues can provide IC analysts and investigators answers as to what substances a body or bodies may have been in contact with at or near death.

With careful observation and collection of data on site, coupled with biological knowledge of the insect concerned, its life cycle, and the external causes involved, such as temperature, rain, and other extreme environmental factors, one can reconstruct the chain of events, including the estimated time of death. In short, the purpose of the forensic entomology discipline in the Intelligence Community is to shed light on the "ground truth" and give a viable estimate, without bias, of the perpetrator's or suspect's "past actions" in human crimes.

The author recommends that a forensic entomologist be called into an investigation at the earliest point, whenever possible. If this is not possible, an entomologist should be consulted before collection of entomological evidence is attempted. The collection of evidence at the death scene (e.g., bodies covered with soot from an improvised explosive device) is the vital link among law enforcement, the assistance of forensic entomologists, and finding the answers for intelligence officials. Such findings could also reveal foul play, and give viable evidence that a body has been deceptively moved in cases of mass graves and genocide. If the evidence is not properly collected, labeled, preserved, or processed, it will yield no forensic value to solving any heinous crime.

Intelligence analysts and law enforcement investigators, scientists, doctors, and researchers are just now beginning to realize how beneficial forensic entomology can be in finding answers involving insects that infest cadavers in different environments and conditions. One of the more important items needed for continued research is better tables of insect development and decaying stages around the world. Tables must be developed under varying environmental conditions with different insect species, and in different locales, domestic and international. This would enable intelligence analysts and law enforcement investigators to estimate PMI in a timely and accurate manner and help solve crimes in an International Criminal Court (ICC) without bias or prejudice.

As with all disciplines of forensic science, forensic entomology continues to evolve. With continuous research in explosive analysis, specifically identifying chemical signatures of explosive compounds and estimating PMI based on entomological evidence, forensic entomology will become even more accurate and more widely accepted around the world. Its ability to provide "ground truth" of an adversary's past actions is not only valuable to the IC, but also to the International Criminal Court (ICC). In the meantime, scientific research has established that insects which metabolize explosive compounds do provide valuable information silently. Forensic scientists, intelligence analysts, law enforcement officials, and local and international courts need only listen to these silent agents and they will learn.

APPENDIX

WEATHER DATA FOR MAY 2004

Today's Date : 26-May-04

May-04 for Washington National, DC (66')   LAT=38.8N LON= 77.0W

| | TEMPERATURE | | | | | | PRECIPITATION | | | |
| | ACTUAL | | | NORMAL | | | | | | |
	HI	LO	AVG	HI	LO	AVG	DEPT	AMNT	SNOW	SNCVR	HDD
1	79	61	70	71	51	61	+9	0.07	0.0	0	0
2	81	57	69	71	51	61	+8	0.67	0.0	0	0
3	57	48	53	72	51	62	-9	0.36	0.0	0	12
4	64	44	54	72	52	62	-8	0.00	0.0	0	11
5	71	49	60	72	52	62	-2	0.41	0.0	0	5
6	76	50	63	72	53	63	+0	0.00	0.0	0	2
7	89	59	74	73	53	63	+11	0.20	0.0	0	0
8	67	56	62	73	53	63	-1	0.00	0.0	0	3
9	83	54	69	73	54	63	+6	trace	0.0	0	0
10	86	64	75	74	54	64	+11	0.01	0.0	0	0
11	89	68	79	74	54	64	+15	trace	0.0	0	0
12	86	68	77	74	55	64	+13	0.00	0.0	0	0
13	85	68	77	74	55	65	+12	0.00	0.0	0	0
14	87	70	79	75	55	65	+14	0.00	0.0	0	0
15	88	67	78	75	56	65	+13	0.15	0.0	0	0
16	81	67	74	75	56	66	+8	0.01	0.0	0	0
17	82	67	75	76	56	66	+9	0.02	0.0	0	0
18	85	67	76	76	56	66	+10	0.05	0.0	0	0
19	79	67	73	76	57	67	+6	0.10	0.0	0	0

HIGHEST TEMPERATURE	92	TOTAL PRECIP		2.55
LOWEST TEMPERATURE	44	TOTAL SNOWFALL		0.0
AVERAGE TEMPERATURE	72.1	NORMAL PRECIP		3.82
DEPARTURE FROM NORM	+7.3	PERCENT OF NORMAL PRECIP		67
HEATING DEGREE DAYS	33			
NORMAL DEGREE DAYS	73			

Key: e= estimated; M= not available; *=tied, most recent year shown

| | TEMPERATURE | | | | | | PRECIPITATION | | | | |
| | ACTUAL | | | NORMAL | | | | | | | |
	HI	LO	AVG	HI	LO	AVG	DEPT	AMNT	SNOW	SNCVR	HDD
20	72	66	69	77	57	67	+2	0.00	0.0	0	0
21	86	68	77	77	57	67	+10	0.04	0.0	0	0
22	89	65	77	77	58	67	+10	trace	0.0	0	0
23	92	74	83	77	58	68	+15	0.00	0.0	0	0
24	90	72	81	78	58	68	+13	0.00	0.0	0	0
25	88	69	79	78	59	68	+11	0.39	0.0	0	0
26	85	69	77	78	59	69	+8	0.07	0.0e	0	0
27	M	M	M	79	59	69	M	M	0.0	0	M
28	M	M	M	79	60	69	M	M	0.0	0	M
29	M	M	M	79	60	70	M	M	0.0	0	M
30	M	M	M	80	60	70	M	M	0.0	0	M
31	M	M	M	80	61	70	M	M	0.0	0	M

TOTALS FOR DCA

HIGHEST TEMPERATURE	92	TOTAL PRECIP	2.55
LOWEST TEMPERATURE	44	TOTAL SNOWFALL	0.0
AVERAGE TEMPERATURE	72.1	NORMAL PRECIP	3.82
DEPARTURE FROM NORM	+7.3	PERCENT OF NORMAL PRECIP	67
HEATING DEGREE DAYS	33		
NORMAL DEGREE DAYS	73		

Key: e= estimated; M= not available; *=tied, most recent year shown

These data were used for determining larvae development during the explosive/larvae metabolization experiment.

Source: *AccuWeather.com*, May 2004, no report number, URL: <http:// www.accuweather.com/adcbin/ public/climo_local.asp?partner=accuweather&zipcode=20535, accessed 26 May 2004.

GLOSSARY

Active decay. That phase of corpse decomposition that follows bloat, is characterized by such maggot activity, and terminates with a rapid decrease in body weight.

Adipocere. A fatty waxy substance resulting from the decomposition of animal corpses in moist places or under water, but not exposed to air.

Advanced decay. That phase of corpse decomposition that follows active decay and is characterized by beetle activity.

Arthropod. Any of the invertebrate animals with jointed appendages, an exoskeleton consisting of chitin and protein, and an open circulatory system.

Bloat. That transient phase in corpse decomposition that follows the fresh phase and is characterized by excessive swelling, produced by gasses trapped internally.

Blowfly. A higher fly in the family of Calliphoridae, also known as bottle flies.

Carrion. Decaying animal flesh.

Community. Used here in an ecological sense, meaning the interacting populations of organisms in a given area.

Cyclorrhapha. The third suborder of Diptera which contains the houseflies, Bluebottles, Greenbottles and their relations.

Diapause. A condition of suspended animation in which development is arrested, usually at a particular stage (prepupae to pupae).

Diel. (Rhythms) within a 24-hour period.

Diurnal. Active in the daytime.

Dried remains. The final phase of corpse decomposition that follows advanced decay and is characterized by little faunal decay.

Eclosion. The process of hatching from the egg or emerging as an adult.

Ecology. The study of the relationships of animals and plants with each other, in communities, and with the physical environment.

Ectoparasite. A parasite that does not completely invade the body, but which feeds superficially on the skin, hair, or feathers or sucks blood.

Endoparasite. A parasite that completely invades the body, i.e., the dermal or subdermal tissues, head cavities, or inner organs.

Face. The area of the head surface bounded by the antennae, compound eyes, and the anterior edge of the mouth opening.

Facultative parasite. An insect or an animal that is normally free living, but which under certain circumstances may lead a parasitic mode of life.

Fauna. Any animal in the animal kingdom.

Flesh fly. A higher fly in the family Sarcophaga haemorrhoidalis.

Forensic entomology. The study of insects and related arthropods from a medical-legal aspect.

Grub. Colloquial name for a larva, usually of the legless maggot type.

Habitat. The locality or situation in which an insect normally lives, or in which development takes place.

Heliotropism. Reaction to the sun; may be positively heliotropic (sun-loving) or negatively heliotropic.

Hypothesis. An unproven theory.

Imago. The adult, sexually-developed insect.

Instar. First stage of fly's life cycle.

Integument. The cuticle or outer covering of the insect's body.

Larva. The active, feeding, immature stage emerging from the egg and differing fundamentally in form from the adult.

Larviparous. Reproducing by bringing forth larvae which have already hatched inside the female reproductive system, such as the flesh fly.

Maggot. A larvae to a higher fly, typical form of Cyclorrhaphous Diptera larva. It sheds its skin twice and has three growth instars prior to pupariation.

Maggot mass. The collective, closely packed mass of higher fly larvae occurring in decomposing carrion.

Medico-legal entomology. Medical entomology from a legal aspect.

Mediterranean climate. Surrounded nearly or completely by land. Used for large bodies of water, such as lakes or seas.

Metamorphosis. The process in arthropods of changing from one life stage into another.

Myiasis. The invasion of any living vertebrate animal by fly larvae.

Necrophagous. Feeding on the dead.

Nematocera. The first of three suborders of Diptera, containing the mostly gnat-like forms (midges, mosquitoes, crane-flies, etc.).

Nymph. The immature feeding stage of insects with an incomplete metamorphosis and resembling a miniature version of the adult.

Obligate parasite. A parasite which is dependent upon its host and which cannot complete its development without its host.

Oviparious. Producing eggs.

Ovipositor. The egg-laying apparatus or genital tube of the female through which oviposition is carried out.

Pabulum. Food of any kind.

Post-feeding larva. The wandering, fasting phase of the 3rd instar larvae, terminating in pupariation.

Postmortem interval. The period of time between death and a corpse discovery.

Pseudomyiasis. A condition in which living or dead dipterous larvae are found in the intestinal tract of living humans and other vertebrate animals.

Ptilinum. Used by the emergent fly to rupture the puparium and to penetrate the pupation medium.

Pupa (pupae). A transformational (metamorphic), but usually immobile, stage between the last larval stage and the adult (imago).

Pupariation. When the post-feeding blowfly larva or white prepupa forms its white puparium that tans and hardens to form the dark brown puparium after about 24 hours.

Puparium (puparia). The thickened, tanned, hardened, barrel-like, last larval skin inside which the pupa of the higher fly is formed.

Pupation. The act of forming the pupa in the process of transforming from the larval stage to the adult.

Putrefaction. The foul-smelling anaerobic decomposition of moist or wet organic matter by microorganisms.

Saponification. The conversion of corpse body fat into curd-like, foul-smelling product.

Saprophagous. Scavengers feeding on dead and decaying organic matter.

Sarcophaga haemorrhoidalis. Red-tailed flesh fly.

Sarcosaprophagous. Feeding on dead flesh.

Scotophelic. Shade-loving.

Seepage. The fluid material draining from the decomposing corpse.

Succession. Used here as ecological succession; the progressive replacement of one ecological community with another.[76]

---

[76] Haskell and Catts, 155-162.

BIBLIOGRAPHY

AccuWeather.com. May 2004. No report number. URL: <http:// www. accuweather.com/ adcbin/public/climo_local.asp?partner=accuweather& zipcode=20535>. Accessed 26 May 2004.

Barenbaum, May R. *Ninety-Nine More Maggots, Mites, and Munchers.* Urbana and Chicago: University of Illinois Press, 1985.

Bianchini, G. "La Biologia Del Cadaver." *Archivic Antropologia Criminale, Psichiatria e Medicina Legale* 50, (1930): 1035-1105.

Bornemissza, F. "An Analysis of Arthropod Succession in Carrion and the Effect of Its Decomposition on the Soil Fauna." *Australian Journal of Zoology* 5 (1957): 1-12.

Bullington, Stephen. "Forensic Entomology." Web-only essay, 24 July 2001. URL: <http:// www.key-net.net/users/swb/forensics>. Accessed 5 January 2004.

Byrd, Jason H. "Forensic Entomology: Insects in Legal Investigations." Web-only essay. URL: <http://www.forensic-entomology.com>. Accessed 5 January 2004.

Byrd, Jason H. Member of American Board of Forensic Entomology. Interview by author, 28 March 2004.

Castner, James L. "Ultimate Guide to Forensic Entomology: A Review of Forensic Identification Cards." Web-only essay. URL: <http://folk.uio.no/mostarke/forens_ent/ reviewFIFC.html>. Accessed 5 January 2004.

Cerilliant Explosive Company. Phone number 1-800-848-7837. Trinitrotoluene (TNT) explosives utilized in explosive entomology project. CAS No 118-96-7. $20.00 plus shipping.

Chang, M. "Fly Witness." *Science World Journal* 54, no. 4, (1997): 8.

Corninski, Lynn, Professor, Sonoma College. "Periodic Table of the Elements." URL: <www.nbsp.sonoma.edu/resouces/teachers_materials/county_regionals/11-03-01/img14.htm>. Accessed 26 May 2004.

Dadour, I. and D. Cook. "Forensic Entomology." Web-only essay. URL: <http:// www.agric.wa.gov.au:7000/ento/forensic.htm>. Accessed 5 January 2004.

"Decomposition: What Happens to the Body After Death? *Australian Museum,* 2003, URL:<http://images.search.yahoo.com/search/images/view?back=http%3a images.search.yahoo.com/search images%3fp=fly%2blife%2bcycle%26ei=UTF8 &h=300&w=500&imgcurl=www.deathonline.net/decomposition/images/lifecycle.jpg&imgurl=www.deathonline.net/decomposition/images/lifecycle.jpg&name=lifecycle.jpg&p=fly+life+cycle&rurl=http%3a// www.deathonline.net/decomposition/corpse_fauna/flies/

life_cycle.htm&rcurl=http%3a//www.deathonline.net/decomposition/ corpse_fauna/flies/life_cycle.htm&type=&no=20&tt=294>. Accessed 9 March 2004.

Emperor's Clothes. "Were NATO's Aerial Photos of Mass Graves Faked?" Web-only essay, Spring and Fall. URL: <http://emperor.vwh.net/misc/graves2.htm>. Accessed 1 June 2004.

"Fatal Aircraft Events Involving U.S. Politicians." *AirSafe.com,* 26 October 2002. *MSN.* Under the keyword "aircraft accidents involving U.S. politicians. URL: <http:// www.cowjones.net/events/celebs/politics.htm>." Accessed 28 April 2004.

Fanning, Michael. Intelligence Analyst at the Federal Bureau of Investigation's (FBI) Hazardous Devices Response Unit, FBI Academy, Quantico, VA. Telephone interview by the author, 8 June 2004.

Ferris, George. CDR, USNR. Chief, Weapons Branch, Joint Intelligence Task Force-Counter Terrorism (JITF-CT), Defense Intelligence Agency (DIA); Special Operations Officer, Explosive Ordnance Disposal (EOD), Washington, DC. Interview by the author, 8 June 2004.

Fisher B. *Techniques of Crime Scene Investigation.* Boca Raton, FL: CRC Press, 1993.

Gail, A. and J. Gaudet. "A Practical Exercise in Forensic Entomology." *RCMP Gazette* 53, no. 11 (1999): 10-14.

Geberth, V. *Practical Homicide Investigation: Tactics, Procedures, and Forensic Techniques.* New York: Boca Raton, 1993.

Gerwehr, Scott and Russell W. Glen. *Unweaving the Web: Deception and Adaptation in the Future Urban Operations.* Monterey, California: Rand, 2002.

Godson, Roy and James J. Wirtz, "Strategic Denial and Deception," in *Strategic Denial and Deception: The 21st Century Challenge.* New Brunswick, NJ: Transaction Publications, 1997.

Grassberger M. and C. Reiter. "Forensic Entomology: Post-Mortem Interval (PMI) Estimation Using Insect Development Data." *Institute of Forensic Medicine, University of Vienna.* URL: <http://www.univie.ac.at/forensic-entomology/ information.htm>. Accessed 9 March 2004.

Guiart, J. "Notices Biographiques II: Francisco Redi 1628-1698." *Archives de Parisitologie* 1, (1898): 420.

Gunatilake, K. and M. L. Goff. "Detection of Organophosphate Poisoning in a Putrefying Body by Analyzing Arthropod Larvae." *Journal of Forensic Sciences* 34 (1989): 3.

Hall, G. *The Blowflies of North America.* Baltimore: Say, 1948.

Hall, Robert D., Ph.D., J.D. Associate Vice Provost for Research, University of Missouri and member of the American Board of Forensic Entomology. Telephone interview by the author, 8 June 2004.

Haskell, Neal H. and E. Paul Catts. *Entomology and Death: A Procedural Guide.* Clemson, South Carolina: Joyce's Print Shop Inc, 1990.

Hilton, Bill Jr. Hilton Pond Center. "June Bug's Gotta Eat Too." Web-only essay, 8-14 July 2002. URL: <www http://images.search.yahoo.com/search/images/ view?back=http%3a//images.search.yahoo.com/search/ images%3fsrch=1%26p= june%2bbeetles%26ei=UTF-8%26n=20%26fl=0&h=365&w= 500& imgcurl =www. hiltonpond.org/images/BeetleJune02.jpg&imgurl=www.hiltonpond.org/ images/BeetleJune02.jpg&name=BeetleJune02.jpg&p=june+bee- tles&rurl=http%3a///www.hiltonpond.org/ThisWeek020708.html&rcurl=http%3a/ /www.hiltonpond.org/ThisWeek020708.html&type=&no=13&tt=417>. Accessed 27 May 2004.

Hobson, P. "Studies of the Nutrition of Blowfly Larvae, III: The Liquefaction of Muscle." *Journal of Experimental Biology* 9 (1932): 359-365.

Introna, F. and others. "Opiate Analysis in Cadaveric Blowfly Larvae as an Indicator of Narcotic Intoxication." *Journal of Forensic Sciences* 35 (1990): 1.

Kebabijan Richard. Aviation Accident Photos. "Wen only essay, 1997-2002. URL: <http://www.planecrashinfo.com/index.html>. Accessed 28 April 2004.

Klapec, George. Forensic Chemist at the Federal Bureau of Alcohol Tobacco and Firearms (ATF), Washington, DC, Office. Telephone interview by the author, 8 June 2004.

Lord, Wayne D. and F. Berger. "Collection and Preservation of Forensically Important Entomological Materials." *Journal of Forensic Sciences* 28 (1983): 936-944.

Lord, Wayne D. and F. Berger. "Arthropods Associated With Harbor Seal (Phoca vitulina) Carcasses Stranded on Island Along the New England Coast." *International Journal of Entomology* 26 (1984): 282-285.

Montagu, Ewan. *The Man Who Never Was: World War II's Boldest Counterintelligence Operation.* Annapolis, Maryland: Naval Institute Press, 1996.

Ohara, J. "Arthropods Associated With Livestock Dung." Web-only essay. URL: <http:// res.agr.ca/ecorc/apss/arthback.htm>. Accessed 8 October 2003.

Oldroyd, H. *Natural History of Flies.* New York: Norton Library, 1964.

Payne, A. "A Summer Carrion Study of the Baby Pig Sus Scrofa Linnaeus." *Ecology* 46, (1965): 592-602.

Rodriguez, William C. III, Ph.D. Chief, Deputy Medical Examiner, Office of the Armed Forces Medical Examiner (AFME), Rockville, MD. Telephone interview by the author, 8 June 2004.

Sachs, J. "A Maggot for the Prosecution." *Discovery* 11 (1998): 103-108.

Sadler, Brent and others. "NATO: Aerial Photo May Show Mass Graves in Kosovo." *CNN*, online ed., 11 April 1999. URL:<http://www.cnn.com/WORLD/europe/9904/11/nato.attack.05/>. Accessed 1 June 2004.

"Serbian Massacres before NATO Airstrikes." *Kosova Crisis Center*. URL:<http://www.alb-net.com/warcrimes-img/warcrimes.htm>. Accessed 9 March 2004.

Smith, K. A *Manual of Forensic Entomology*. New York: Cornell University Press, 1986.

Starkeby, M. "Ultimate Guide to Forensic Entomology: Introduction to Forensic Entomology." Web-only essay. URL< http://folk.uio.no/mostarke/forens_ent/ introduction.shtml>. Accessed 5 January 2004.

Tandahl, Jeff. "The USA Patriot Act." Electronic Privacy Information Center. URL: <http://www.epic.org/privacy/terrorism/usapatriot/>. Accessed 8 June 2004.

U.S. Department of Justice, Federal Bureau of Investigation. *"FBI Director Mueller Announces Five New Computer Forensic Laboratories."* Washington: FBI National Press Office, 8 October 2003. URL: <http://www.fbi.gov/pressrel/pressrel03/lab100803.htm>. Accessed 9 June 2004.

Webster's II *New Riverside University Dictionary*, 2nd ed., 1984.

ABOUT THE AUTHOR

Lieutenant Albert M. Cruz enlisted in the U.S. Navy in 1990. Following basic training and Aircrew Survival Equipment School, he served with VAW-113, Naval Air Station (NAS) Miramar; HS-8, NAS North Island; and Explosive Ordnance Disposal (EOD) MU-3 and SEAL Team FIVE at Naval Amphibious Base, Coronado, California. In 1997, after being appointed as a Special Operations Rigger, he was selected for the prestigious Enlisted Education Advancement Program (EEAP) for enlisted sailors and graduated with a Bachelor of Science in Criminal Justice from National University, San Diego, California. His graduate education includes a Master of Forensic Sciences (MFS) from National University and a Master of Science of Strategic Intelligence (MSSI) with a concentration in Denial and Deception (D&D) from the then-Joint Military Intelligence College (JMIC) in Washington, D.C.

LT Cruz attended Officer Candidate School (OCS) as a Special Operations Officer and was commissioned an Ensign in 2000. Upon completing OCS, he attended Surface Warfare School at SWOSCOLCOM in Newport, Rhode Island, and Dive Officer training at NAVDIVSALTRACEN, Panama City Beach, Florida. In October 2001, he reported to the USS SALVOR at Pearl Harbor, Hawaii, and was assigned as Operations Officer, Dive Officer, Air Operations Officer, Antiterrorism/Force Protection Officer, and Intelligence Officer. In 2004 he graduated from JMIC with orders to NAVSCOLEOD, where he earned his demolition qualification. In 2006, he was selected as a Foreign Area Officer and is considered a "Plank Owner" in the newly developed Navy HUMINT designator. He is currently serving as Flag Aide to the Commander, U.S. Naval Forces South, in Mayport, Florida.

LT Cruz has served on the staff of Congressman Brian P. Bilbray of San Diego and for the Superior Court of California. In addition, he has deployed to Asia, the Middle East, and Central and South America where he has conducted many high-risk air and dive operations. Operations both in the U.S. and abroad in which he has been involved include the Ehime Maru Project, USS MISSISSINEWA Project, Cooperative Afloat Readiness and Training 2002, Operation TEAMWORK SOUTH, Operation BEL SUBMARINO 1996 and 1998, Operation SOUTHERN WATCH 1993, and several Chief of Naval Operations (CNO) special projects. Most recently, he participated in Exercise UNITAS 2006, during which U.S. maritime units circumnavigated the continent of South America conducting joint and combined operations with allied forces from a number of different nations.

www.ingramcontent.com/pod-product-compliance
Lightning Source LLC
Chambersburg PA
CBHW070105300526
45788CB00016B/2458